THE HOMESCHOOLING PARENT TEACHES *MATH!*

Bringing Math to the Math-Averse

(Parents and Kids Both!)

Kerridwen Mangala McNamara, M.S.

Ivory Tower Lair
An Imprint of Rising Dragon Books

The Homeschooling Parent: Brinigng Math to the Math-Averse (Parents and Kids Both!)
Copyright © 2023 by Kerridwen Mangala McNamara
Published by Ivory Tower Lair, an imprint of Rising Dragon Books.
Cover art and illustrations by the author.
Book and Cover design by author.
168 pages
For further information, email RisingDragonBooks@gmail.com
ISBN (pbk): 978-1-960160-21-8
ISBN (eBook): 978-1-960160-20-1

ISBN: 978-1-960160-21-8
First Print Edition: November 2023
10 9 8 7 6 5 4 3 2 1

For my dad, Dr. Suresh K, Bhate, Ph.D.,
who made me learn the Math in the first place.

For my husband, who had faith in my ability to
homeschool our kids and teach them math
even when I didn't always have it for myself...
and who engaged with me in the greatest marketing
scheme since "Move to Greenland - the climate is great!"

For my kids, who made me have to fake confidence and
enthusiasm for math for long enough that it
became REAL.

And for my oldest daughter, A. Meenakshi McNamara,
who gave me the opportunity to realize
Math could be enjoyable.

CONTENTS

KERRIDWEN MANGALA McNAMARA

Introduction

From a Mom's Perspective...

"**M**ATH IS SOOOOO BOOORING..."
"Math is too hard."

"I hate math!"

Every parent has heard these things, including me.

The real story behind those complaints is that math is *scary* to a great many people. Some of those people are kids.

But a great many of those people are grown-ups: parents and teachers; and we transmit our own fears and negative math experiences to our kids, even when we don't mean to.

Okay, so you knew all that before you picked up this book. Why should you keep reading?

This book is about changing our relationships with math. The relationships our *kids* have with math *and* the relationship we have with math ourselves. Our ultimate goal is not to transform ourselves into math-lovers, but to go somewhat beyond math-tolerators to become math-*appreciators*.

1

We do this by creating a *math-positive environment* in our families and in our lives.

Why bother?

Well, some of the benefits might be immediately obvious – less fighting and better grades (or progress) for your kids. Other benefits - to yourself and your family and even your community – might seem more nebulous or pie-in-the-sky, but it's possible that you'll appreciate them even more in the long run.

How do I know?

I was afraid of math for a long time, *even though I got good grades in it.*

I thought I sucked at math because my good grades "weren't all my own work" since I had other people helping me or tutoring me along the way. I went farther with math than most people do – even most people in my chosen STEM-field (I'm a biologist) – and I *still* thought I sucked at math.

It wasn't until I was 40 years old and my oldest daughter was thirteen and beginning to really love math (for reasons I'm still unclear about). It didn't last for much longer – she sped ahead at lightspeed – but I suddenly realized I was *good* at math because I could answer the more advanced questions she was working on, even though it took some effort.

It took me another *three* years – and creating a "Math Circle" to try to build a supportive community for her – to realize I *like* math.

And… when I say I "like" math I don't mean that I go around looking for math puzzles to solve (I actually kind of hate those). It doesn't mean that I can solve problems that I solved way back in college anymore (doing calculus and differential equations is NOT like riding a bike, I'm disappointed to tell you). And it doesn't mean I think everyone should go "Yippee!" when someone has a math question.

Heck no.

For me "liking math" means I'm not *scared* of it anymore.

It means that I don't cringe over setting up a spreadsheet to track my words written or my household expenses (though I may be cringing for other reasons). It means I don't avoid helping my husband with the taxes (though 2021 taxes were some weird labyrinth, even for a normal 1040). It means that I feel a certain confidence that I *can* solve both my kids' academic questions and help them understand... and that I can solve real-world problems like how much tile to buy for the bathroom floor or how much wood we need for that A-frame goat-shelter we built last year.

It means that when I read an article that mentions statistics or the federal budget or estimates of how many stars are in the universe – or whatever – I can decide whether I'm going to stop and think through their argument more closely or just keep reading. I usually just keep reading, but I have the confidence that I can go back and untangle what they meant or even decide I think the author was wrong if I end up caring to take the time.

It means that I can look around the world and see a different kind of beauty. (And for me that means a different and deeper kind of connection to the Universe... this book isn't about that, though, so we'll leave those musings for another day).

And it means that I was able to *support* my daughter to retain *her* enthusiasm for mathematics. And it worked! She's about to start applying to graduate schools in mathematics! (Before you freak out, none of the other five kids seem to think of math as more than somewhat interesting and useful and tolerable... *mostly* tolerable.)

But lastly... it means that when my daughter tells me about some exciting thing she's learned or is working on in math... I don't always *understand,* but I can ask questions and get something out of it enough that she *keeps coming back to talk to me.*

And as parents, that's a big part of our goal – with math or otherwise. We want our battles over math – or writing or reading or history or whatever – to still, somehow, end with our kids both knowledgeable about the subject and capable of using it at whatever level they are going to need it in their grown-up lives... But also, that they don't see us as those screeching monsters who forced them to do this thing they hated (even if they now appreciate knowing it). We want them to call us up randomly out of the blue to chat and tell us about their lives and ask us questions and listen to our lives. We want them to appreciate us, and for that appreciation not to be marred by traumatic memories of battles over math.

In this book, I'll share some of my personal math journey, and that of some of my kids. Mostly I'll refer to them by the ages they were at the time or by "code-names" to avoid personal embarrassments. (I'll likewise keep the stories from friends and other homeschoolers that I have been gifted to observe largely anonymized.) It was a *rocky* journey, even for people who actually came from relatively math-positive (but rather different) families as my husband and I both did.

But in the end... sharp rocks and tears along the way or not, if the cuts and bruises got kisses and hugs and you can look back on the vista behind and say "wow!" and look at each other and say "that was cool, let's do it again!" ...it was worth it to us.

Hopefully this book can show you a somewhat smoother path to the peak!

(And if what you need right now is just a list of resources... you can skip straight to the back! So long as you keep in mind that a resource is only as helpful as you make it...)

THE HOMESCHOOLING PARENT TEACHES *MATH!*

Chapter One:

How NOT to teach math

- **You don't have to follow current or former school approaches**
- **You don't have to stick to the first curriculum (that you try)**
- **You don't have to use a curriculum (with a caveat)**

MY PARENTS LOVED MATH. THEY were those annoying kids in school who thrived on testing and pop-quizzes. They adored "drill and kill" approaches because they excelled at them. And they expected me to do the same. When they pulled me out of school for health reasons and bullying (described in some detail in my first book *The Homeschooling Parent*) at the beginning of second grade, they were deeply invested in me continuing to take the standardized tests at the end of the year – and they turned what the school seemed to use as a simple evaluation into *high-stakes testing* by telling me that if I didn't do "well enough" we were giving up the "homeschooling experiment" and sending me back to school. For me, school meant bullying (the emotional kind that wasn't really considered bullying in the very early '80s, so my parents weren't entirely aware) and for them, "well enough" meant better than the 95th percentile.

Parental expectations will do a lot, and I did my best.

But I hated it.

Let me be clear: I don't harbor any resentment towards my parents for any of this. They did an amazing job in my entirely-biased opinion, including making the very hard decision to homeschool when, literally, *nobody* outside of certain very Right-wing religious groups or very, *very* Left-wing communities was doing it. There were no curricula, no support groups, no playgroups, no co-ops, and no *information* besides a strict school-at-home approach or unschooling.

My parents were brave and, without exaggeration, may have saved my life. They certainly saved my sanity.

And they taught me in the way that had worked for them, which is an entirely legit way to approach the question.

My mind works enough the way theirs does that I could learn like this… but school's drill-and-kill-and-God-help-you-if-you-get-it-wrong approach had just about destroyed my interest in math. Now I saw it as a necessary, if somewhat horrible, thing I had to do to get to keep homeschooling, so I approached math with a certain grim intensity when need be and avoided it like the plague the rest of the time.

What my parents didn't know was this:

You don't have to follow current or former school approaches

This is both the most utterly freeing and most utterly terrifying thing to hear.

You don't have to teach or learn the way you learned it. Or the way your friend who homeschools does it. Or the way your homeschool co-op families do it.

Or the way your local school district (or state, or even *country*) does it.

There's a caveat to this, of course.

Depending on where you live, there may be local, state, or federal regulations on what (and in a few places, even *how*) you homeschool or teach specific subjects. If there are such regulations in your area, Math is probably the first topic regulated, for all that very, very few schools do a particularly good job with it. Your first job as the homeschooling parent is always to look up what regulations you need to meet (and which ones are "recommended" but not required); I advise you to contact your nearest Unschooling group or Waldorf School if you disagree with those regulations and find out how they get around those regulations… at least in the United States, my understanding is that it is legal to Unschool in all the states, so there has to be a way.

Okay, now that the "I'm not a lawyer, please do your research" caveat has been discussed… back to the topic.

You probably learned math in school the way most of us did in school. Your teacher presented a particular type of problem and then made you do hundreds and hundreds of variations on that problem. By the time you were done with all that, and she was ready to move on to the next one, you were *really, really good* at solving that one type of problem… but most of us probably couldn't take a curve-ball where the problem was presented a little differently, or where we had to use that kind of problem to solve something in the real world.

And if you didn't figure out how to solve that *one* type of problem… the answer was usually to load you with *more* of that kind of problem in some sort of hope of hammering it into your head until it stayed, even if you didn't understand (or, by this point, *care*) about solving it at all.

And then, once you'd done a few rounds of this sort of thing, there would be the Review and the Exam and you had to pry all the old types of problems back out (after they'd been hammered down beneath new layers of other ones) and hopefully be able to solve them well enough to get a good grade.

This method is often called "Drill-and-Kill" – and it *does* have a few benefits.

One benefit is that most of us know how to operate this way. This is how *we* were taught, so it's the natural approach for many of us to start with. It feels… well, maybe not *comfortable,* but familiar. And, honestly, familiarity – especially when you are first embarking into the world of homeschooling – is not to be underestimated.

A second benefit is that it's easy to find resources for this approach. Kumon (both the "after-school" institutions and the workbooks you'll find at Barnes & Noble) and the popular Saxon homeschooling curriculum are a couple of examples of this. Math-aids.com is a website that allows you to generate customized worksheets with lots of problems – so you could use it for this approach as well (but also in other ways, more on that later).

But the *biggest* benefit of "Drill-and-Kill" in my experience to-date is that it makes you get incredibly *fast* at very specific types of problems. You get *fast* because you are really memorizing those specific problems *and their answers* and then when you see them again – possibly even in a different context, which is the real goal – you can spit out the answer, move on, and accomplish something else faster than if you had to sort it all out.

And, yes, the *faster* thing, really is a Thing. And not just in elementary (or middle or high) school.

Why?

Because while math isn't quite as sequential as we're usually taught (I'm getting to that…) each bit of it *does* build on the parts you already know. If you have to stop and count on your fingers every time you hit an addition problem under 10 – or do the "trick" of adding/subtracting instead of multiplying/dividing – it's going to slow you down when you get to Algebra. And then *that* is going to slow you down in Physics or Chemistry or Personal Finance or even Home Economics (baking, for example, and doubling or halving recipes). Or Carpentry, Costume Design, or Garden-planning.

You know, at things you *(or your kid)* might actually care about.

And being slow at something you care about is *frustrating*.

And *frustration* is what we are trying to take out of math, not intentionally put into it.

My oldest daughter, Meenakshi, is a mathematician and, unarguably, *better* at all kinds of math than her dad (who is a professor of electrical engineering and uses pretty advanced math daily). However, she is *slower* than he is at basic arithmetic... and, depending on how we set it up, she's even slower than I am.

Now this isn't necessarily a fair comparison. The TV show "Are You Smarter Than a Fifth Grader" pitted actual fifth graders against adults who hadn't looked at the material the kids had just finished learning in twenty years or more. Meenakshi doesn't bother with arithmetic anymore – she's doing some exotic thing called "Operator Algebras". So, she might be a bit out of practice.

Her dad and I are still faster than *our* fifth grader – and our seventh grader, for that matter – on basic arithmetic. And our fifth and seventh graders are really *good* at math.

The difference is that we didn't do "Drill-and-Kill" with our kids, although we were subjected to it ourselves as children.

Now, the *downsides* of "Drill-and-Kill" are beyond obvious. It's boring, it's disconnected from the real world, and – unless you are the type of person who thrives on repetition or have a teacher who gives you a great amount of useful feedback on your mistakes – pretty discouraging.

Great teachers – and there are a lot of them out there – have spent the last twenty (or thirty… or forty) years trying to find ways to make Math more connected and connectable. Among the various tools they have explored are different Learning Styles, Problem-Based (or Project-Based) Learning, Gameschooling (not what school teachers call it, but it is what it is), and Consumer (or Real World) Math. Everyone seems to realize that there is a problem with how math is taught and learned – nobody is happy with the aggregate statistics for their national education systems (except maybe Singapore, more on them later).

This is where all this New Math and (in the USA) Common Core comes from. The Educational Establishment is trying to Make Math More Accessible and Absorbable.

And it's a monumental task.

Well.

It is if you are trying to deal with (in the USA) 50-60 *million* kids.

And if you are trying to use the same curriculum for every single one of them. (Or, perhaps, modify it slightly for the kids who fall too far off the center of the Bell curve on either end.)

But it's an entirely solvable problem for homeschoolers.

Why?

Because you only have one or two or a handful of kids. (I have six, and I know a few people with more than me.)

Because you don't have to buy (or find free online) the *one* state- or federally-approved curriculum… and buy three hundred copies of it from the publisher… and then try to push and shove it into a shape that works better for the twenty percent or so of kids at either end of your classroom learning curve… and just wince helplessly at the twenty to forty percent of kids for whom it *sort of* works, but not terribly well. And then work like the dickens to get it to work for everyone, because if all your kids aren't up to an arbitrarily decided 'grade-level' by the end of the school year, it could mean your job, no matter where each of them started, and no matter how much they improved from that starting point.

Which brings me to the next point:

You don't have to stick to the first curriculum (that you try)

YOU, the HOMESCHOOLING PARENT can purchase your curriculum one year, one semester, or even *one workbook* at a time and see if it's a good fit for your *one* child who's at that level. (Or your two or whatever if you have twins, or two kids who happen to be on the some level.)

YOU, the HOMESCHOOLING PARENT can *ditch your little piece of curriculum* if it is clearly not working for both you *and* your kid… after a year, a semester, even a month. (I suggest giving anything a month.) There are lots of places to sell gently-used homeschool curriculum – from Craigslist and eBay to specialty websites and, if you're lucky, even local brick-and-mortar stores (usually run by some homeschooling parent – or former homeschooling parent – which rocks, because he or she can tell you about other curricula they have seen that might meet your needs better).

Do you take a loss on re-selling? Of course, but it's not as big a hit as you might expect if your stuff is in good shape (even several years later, when you're done with it, instead of just jumping ships), and if you buy the *smallest* bit of the curriculum that the publisher will sell you that you think you'll use (say a single workbook and/or textbook… and *maybe* the solutions manual or teacher's guide) then it's a smaller loss to try something out. The curriculum that you loathed or your kid burst into tears over (or vice versa… or both) might be a perfect fit for someone else. And vice versa, so check those used sources yourself!

YOU, the HOMESCHOOLING PARENT can use a *different* curriculum for each of the kids in your care. Or you can use that one copy you bought for Child #1 for the next two and switch for Child #4. Or you can loan or give it away to a friend. (Or if it's one that you hated, to someone you dislike… I suppose..)

YOU, the HOMESCHOOLING PARENT can decide *how* and *how much* to use the curriculum you bought. If you decided to go rock-bottom cheap and pick up the Kumon (or Star Wars) workbooks at Barnes & Noble (yes, there really are Star Wars-themed workbooks for math and English… they're not bad, but only younger grades), but you've gotten excited about Gameschooling… You can decide to take you're kid out to the trampoline and have them jump the answers to the Kumon workbook (I wouldn't suggest this with 3-digit by 2-digit multiplication… unless your kid is *really* energetic and you have a *lot* of time) or get out your Star Wars Legos and line them up to solve the math problems before (re)building the Death Star or Millenium Falcon.

You can also, as I ended up doing, *skip all the Exercises* and just have your kid do the Reviews so long as they're meeting your standard to move on. (Often that's about 80% correct. Some families – or some kids – like to go back and fix any errors. I have two right now who work that way. Others are satisfied if the errors look like careless mistakes, but all the concepts being 'reviewed' are getting a similar level of accuracy. I've gone back and forth on this.)

YOU HAVE THE CONTROL.

And if that means using a video-based approach for Child #1 (like Khan Academy), a game-based approach for Child #2 (like ProdigyGameOnline), and woodworking with Child #3 – but you have all of them do the Reviews in a Singapore workbook (or do the Math Kangaroo competition) just to see where they would compare with other kids of their age or grade… *THAT IS OKAY.*

Why am I harping on this point?

Because the **NUMBER ONE** stress that I see homeschoolers – especially, but not only brand-new ones – struggling with is this idea that the curriculum is THERE. You BOUGHT IT. Now you must USE IT. And you have to USE IT THE WAY THEY TELL YOU.

No.

You don't.

Except for certain very special circumstances, there are no Curriculum Police making sure your kid does every last, painful page of that curriculum that makes you both feel more than slightly nauseous. Or makes one of you throw tantrums to avoid it (we won't talk about whether that would be you or the kid). Those special circumstances occur when you have either *chosen* to use a curriculum that comes with oversight (online or in-person) or if you live in one of the areas where a particular curriculum is government-mandated (and they check up on it) …or if you have custody issues going on and need to satisfy a non- or partially-custodial parent or guardian that you are meeting some mutually agreed-upon standard for your kids' education.

All of these things have their place: some of us thrive on the "accountability" of these bought curricula, some of us trust the government-chosen curriculum, and in the case of a custody situation, sometimes you're compromising on curriculum but getting to homeschool the kids and that's a win right there.

But if you are *not* tied into one of these special situations (and remember, if it's a curriculum you bought, you can *ditch* it!) then you have the flexibility to be creative to meet your kids' needs.

How creative?

Well, in the extreme…

You don't have to use a curriculum (with a caveat)

In the *absolute* extreme, this is called Unschooling (or even *Radical* Unschooling). And, to be quite honest, most of us aren't there. Unschooling is a philosophical choice based on the idea that kids will learn what they need when *they* need to learn it. And that's all well and good, and it *can* work… except that for Unschooling to work *well* requires a tremendous amount more effort from the homeschooling parent.

Why? Because it's not about letting your kids just run around like wild animals all day. It's about providing a very Learning Positive Environment, such that they are constantly seeing things that excite and interest them and that they want to explore further. It's about being very, *very* aware of how much you can nudge and suggest before *their* interest becomes *your* interest and you are dragging them to go see more dinosaurs or whatever and they now hate dinosaurs. And it's about being incredibly *patient* and *trusting in (whatever you put your trust in)* that this will all work out in the end and you won't end up with a 20-year-old (or 30-year-old) eating you out of house and home and lying around watching videos all day long. (Though since that particular outcome seems to come out of public/private school education as well…??)

An "unschool-y" approach can be very workable in the younger years, however.

Quite honestly, there really isn't anything sacred about learning addition in kindergarten, subtraction in first grade, multiplication in second, and division in third. The Waldorf School approach introduces all four of those operations *simultaneously* in first grade and continues growing them each year, just as one example of doing it differently. And the ancient Greeks didn't have modern arithmetic in the same way – their focus was entirely on Geometry. And one of the reasons the USA tried (only semi-successfully) to introduce Common Core was because different school districts around the country taught (or teach) things in different sequences, so a kid who ended up moving a couple times might cover fractions three times and miss percentages entirely (this is actually one of the reasons so many military families homeschool, since most of them move every couple of years).

If you choose to go "curriculum free"…you may still find yourself using the odd piece of a bought (or printed-off-the-internet, or videos, or…) curriculum.

Why?

Because there are some really awesome resources out there, many of which are *free*.

Because it is a *pain-and-a-half* to create *all* your own curriculum from scratch (so sayeth the voice of experience).

And finally, because, you have other things to do with your life than plan out solvable math problems and concoct elaborate and sneaky ways to get your kids to do math.

Seriously, people. Someone else has already done that work. Even if you consider yourself (or would like to) an Unschooling family… it is *not* "cheating" to use someone else's prepared materials.

I actually prefer the term **CHILD-INSPIRED** to the more commonly used "unschooling".

The kids *inspire* our homeschooling approach by letting me and their dad (and older siblings) know what they find exciting and interesting. They may or may not have some long-term "career" goal or "this is how I want to change the world" goal. But they almost *never* have any idea how to get to where they want to go, even if they know where that is.

My job, as the parent, is to do the research and talk to people and *find the resources*. This means helping them figure out where they are going, and helping them map out potential futures where they have control over their own lives (and pay for their own food). It also means figuring out what are some of the possible paths to getting to those endpoints – and helping the kids see that there are certain things they need to do to get to their desired outcome.

We never see *all* the possible paths, of course, and we have to be open to the idea that the kid may change their mind in mid-stream. My oldest daughter was gung-ho about dinosaurs from age 3 to age 12 – at which point she ran out of kids' books and there was a gap where the next level of books was about the paleontologists' life stories (which she couldn't care less about at that time) and then college-level texts on dinosaur anatomy and behavior and so on. She gave up on dinosaurs (despite the *vast* collection of miniatures which still fills out house and has been largely adopted by younger siblings), spent a couple years playing around with other ideas, and ended up becoming enchanted with Math and Physics. (Trust me, this was a *huge* surprise.) In this whole process I had to get over *my* attachment to her interest in paleontology. (It also threw her next two siblings for a loop. They had spent six or eight years planning how their interests – insects and vehicles – could work with hers and they would all go on digs together.)

What we *do* see are the things the kids can't... or won't.

Such as, that they need math for whatever future they are going to be living. Life is a great deal *cheaper* if you don't have to hire an accountant to do your taxes, you know how to budget, and you can halve or double a recipe, just to name a few things. Life is a great deal more *fun* if you can plan a vacation (logistics is a branch of math... and so is finance so you can afford to go), or outwit that snarky computer-game because you know the likelihood (the *probability*) of a mob spawning near your castle.

And, of course, life can be a great deal more *interesting* if you have enough tools so that you aren't always stuck doing someone else's bidding and you can take opportunities that are more exciting because you have the skills to do it. Math is only one of the skills you need... but as our world gets techier and techier... it's not really a skill we can afford to ignore.

Or afford to hate. Because what we *hate* we avoid or forget or procrastinate or get scared or angry at. And none of those things get us anywhere useful, fun, or interesting.

So… bottom-line?

Let your homeschooling be Child-Inspired. Follow their interests, but guide their path using whatever tools work for your family — strict curriculum, loose curriculum, partial curriculum, *maybe* even no curriculum (but be careful to make sure "no curriculum" doesn't mean "no learning" …more on that coming up, too!)

But don't forget:

- **You don't have to follow current or former school approaches**
- **You don't have to stick to the first curriculum (that you try)**
- **You don't have to use a curriculum (with a caveat)**

Chapter Two:

Comparing Curricula
(matching you and your kids' needs to what's available)

- Philosophical choices
- Learning styles: visual/ hands on/ desk work
- Online curricula (do they work?)
- Different amounts of parent-child interaction/ input
- Cost

So... NOW WHAT?

I just told you that you have COMPLETE CONTROL over your curriculum, including whether or not to use one.

That... just leaves you out there hanging.

So, let's take a look at how curricula work and see if we can find something that works for you and your kid. Or kids, plural. Keep in mind that you *might* need different curricula for different kids *in your family.*

This is part of why school teachers' jobs are so hard. While you *might* – with a great deal of effort on your part – manage to shoehorn Child #2 into curriculum you know and familiar with (big pluses, honestly) if it's not a great fit for her, but it was like a glove for her big sister... can you imagine doing that for *thirty* kids?

I can't. I really, really can't, and my hat is off to every man or woman who steps into a classroom and tries to do that every day. Most of them are dedicated to trying to make what they have work for everyone – including buying extra supplies out of their own pockets and finding extra time (taken from their families) to do that. It's not a surprise to me that so many of them burn out, get frustrated and bitter, and so on. The miracle is that there are still so many of them who are awesome, loving teachers right up to the day they retire.

Back to our problem, however.

The first things to do are to figure out:

1. How much time you can devote to this – both time with your kid as well as time spent prepping and grading/evaluating

2. What your budget is

3. What your kid's *and your own* Learning Styles are

4. Where you are philosophically (right now) on homeschooling.

To be absolutely, cruelly, honest... no one has answers to any of those things when they get started.

No one.

Not that oh-so-together-seeming mom at your co-op. Not the one who looks frazzled (but has a kid winning STEM awards) at your playgroup. Not the teacher who lives across the street from you (even if they just got their degree and are certified in all the latest techniques, even if they were *your* teacher and have thirty years of experience under their belt). Not your mom or dad or Uncle Joe. Not your ever-loving spouse or parenting-partner (who is, hopefully, also your *homeschooling* partner, but we all know that the effort at making this work is rarely evenly distributed).

That said, any of these people may have very useful things to say, suggestions, things they have noticed about you and your kids… and so on.

Listen. But don't just follow what they say to do.

If you are just getting started, you should be considering a "deschooling" period – use that time to research what your options are. (And, yes, deschooling is very, very important and will bite you in the butt if you try to skip it entirely. For those of you starting at the beginning of a new school-year, the summer before *might* suffice. But even if you are pulling your kid out mid-year and you have to meet some arbitrary assessment at the end of the year... you absolutely *have* to give yourself and your kid some time to get used to the new venue of homeschooling. See my previous book, *The Homeschooling Parent* for a more in-depth discussion.)

If you are a "veteran" homeschooler who is reading this book to try to reduce some of the tension around Math in your home and build a more Math Positive Environment… you, too, may need to "rest" or "deschool" math for a bit. While you and your kid are used to homeschooling, there's some Math-vibe going that isn't a happy one… and you need to make a clean break and give yourself a chance to come at it with a fresh attitude.

TRUE STORY

One my mom-friends was homeschooling her highly math-Gifted (but not math-loving) only child. She and her husband are both very STEM-y, Math-y people (scientists) and they had been going full-steam ahead with what is probably the most *intense* homeschooling program I've ever seen. I would honestly – as an adult –

love to have been their student, what with all the cool, deep explorations of History, English, Science, Geography... Wow! And her kid was eating it up! (I had to be careful not to tell my kids too many details... because there is *no way* I could have sustained that kind of effort...)

But her son (at age 8 or so) was starting to push back against the Math... despite picking things up easily and well and being a couple grades ahead of his age.

The mom and I discussed this every month at our Homeschool Parent Support Group meeting for... oh, six-ish months. At this point my oldest daughter was applying for colleges as a Math-major-to-be and my other kids did Math competitions, I ran a Math Circle... I had some "street-cred" with Math, even with as accomplished and driven a mom as this one.

But this other mom's solution still floored me, for all that it was absolutely brilliant (like her... yeah, she'll probably be reading this book, LOL).

She decided to "rest" Math for awhile. And her "awhile" ended up being over 6 months.

No more fights.

They went on to work more on other things that the 8yo was excited about – music composition, for example – and continued on with their History, English, and so on.

And eventually their son started asking to do Math.

And when he came back to it – after a little review to remind him of where they'd left off – he was surging ahead again with enthusiasm and no more fights. (He's a kid, I'll assume there were still some complaints, but not *fights*).

Of course, it *helped* that the kid I describe in the side-bar is Gifted in Math and that he was already "ahead" when they took their "rest"… but it *also* helped that he was *eight*. (I saw another mom do this — her son was more like twelve… and he's now eighteen and a math major in college… and graduating early.)

Just for the record, *I've* never been that brave when it came to math — though we've taken 'unofficial' breaks from English, Science, History, or… pretty much anything else.

One of the other hardest things for us homeschooling parents to wrap our heads around is that *there is no race to the finish line.*

You can *choose* to have your kids compete, take standardized tests (unless you live where they are mandated), or participate in other evaluations. You can *choose* to compare your kid to Ava and Liam across the street.

But — unless you are planning to enroll that kid in a school next year — if your kid is in the Elementary grades, or even Middle School grades, there is time to take a break. It's a little hairier in the High School Years… but you can do it then, too, if need be.

And it is always, always, *always* more productive to stop an unproductive activity (or curriculum) and take a breather to re-evaluate. It is *far* better to do that than to build (or keep building) a deep and abiding hatred or phobia of the subject — whether it's Math, Spelling, or History.

Take the time, take a breather, and find a more sustainable and enjoyable way to accomplish that subject area. More enjoyable for you, your kid, and your family at-large.

Okay, off my soapbox.

I'm going to start with the easiest part of this first.

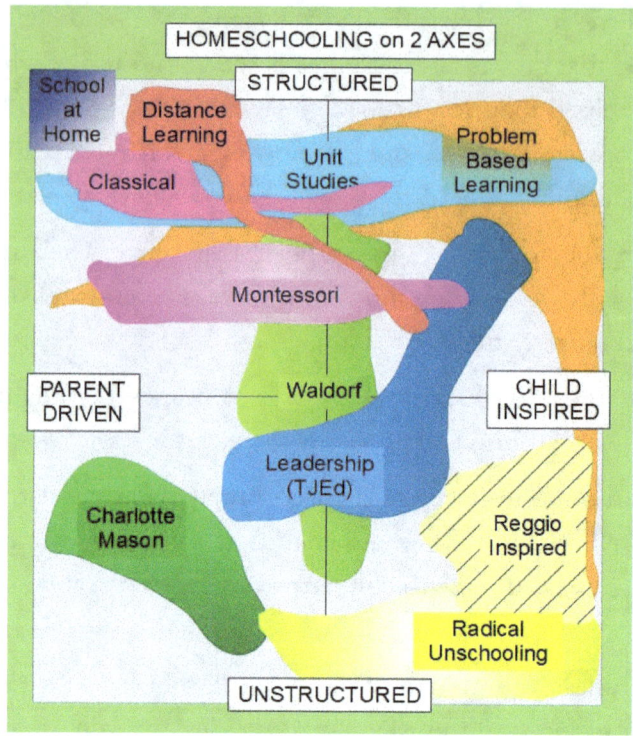

Philosophical choices

The accompanying graphic puts your choices on two axes. You can have varying amounts of Structure and you can have varying amounts of Parent/Child input into choices and planning. Every family will sit at a somewhat different area on this chart – and many will migrate around a bit, or choose different regions for different subjects or different areas of life. My family wanders around mostly in the upper right quadrant, but we have been known to move farther left into Parent-Driven territory at times.

Most of these areas are not really mutually exclusive, and – as you can tell by the blobby labeled shapes – there's a great deal of overlap in the schools of thought that might be placed on this chart.

Why have I given this to you? Because if you have some idea where you are, it can give you a start at hunting for appropriate resources. If, for example, you think you're smack-dab in the middle, that's

Waldorf, and you can read a little about how Waldorf-homeschoolers (or Waldorf schools) do their thing. Slightly "northwest" of the center, but still in the middle? A Waldorf-based curriculum that has grown closer to Common Core might be OakMeadow (a whole curriculum… but also available piecemeal).

Common Core would be that top left corner labeled "School at Home" – and I don't recommend trying to hang out there. In my experience that corner is the hardest one for the parent to sustain, and the least likely way to see the changes you were hoping for when you decided to homeschool. Most parents of my acquaintance who have stayed up there end up sending their kids back to school… not always willingly, but out of desperation and frustration. It's just too constricting.

Likewise, the bottom right corner (Radical Unschooling) has some problems as discussed in the previous chapter. It can be made to work – like School at Home – but both of these are the most parent-intensive approaches when done effectively, although for opposite reasons. (In School at Home, the parent organizes and plans *everything*. In Radical Unschooling the parent needs to be ready to hop and change directions instantaneously as the child's attention shifts. I've also *tried* both and they are *exhausting*.)

You can come back to this chart to give you ideas about what new schools of thought you might want to pursue as you and your homeschooling family change and grow.

Next up is…

Learning styles: visual/ hands on/ desk work

How does your kid learn best? How do *you* learn best? How do you *teach* best?

These are all different questions, and it might take some trial and error to figure out the answers to them. You need to find a curriculum that meets what works for *them* with what works for *you*.

For example, in my previous incarnation as a research scientist (BC = Before Children) I learned that I am… not great at bench-science. Meaning *doing experiments*. I just don't have the meticulous patience to do experiments such that I can be sure that the results answer what I'm asking. It took me *nine years* of college and grad school to figure this out… and I learned a great many wonderful things, made a great many wonderful friends, met my spouse of 26 years and counting… but bench-science and I were a terrible match and I made myself seriously ill before I accepted this and quit my Ph.D. program.

And… all of that (being sick and always, always, always struggling to accomplish what everyone else used as "easy" breaks when their tough stuff wasn't working) left me with a great dislike for doing experiments. Or, really, *most* "hands-on" stuff.

I'm a visual learner for the most part – I can read a book, maybe work some problems, and I'm good. I can teach it to someone else, or use it when I need it. (Ironically, I'm also a *kinesthetic* learner in the sense of being a dancer. Didn't carry over into the lab, more's the pity.)

My Child #1 is also primarily a visual learner… but she's more evenly good at learning physically and through sound, like lectures. She worked herself through most textbooks with only a bit of help from me and we didn't realize that she loved when I read to her because of the audio-component being important until she started taking college classes and absolutely *adored* the lectures.

Children #s 2, 3, and 4, however, are very distinctly audio-/hands-on- learners.

This… drove me crazy.

I realized relatively early on that they absorbed things better if I read the material aloud. And, with such a large number of kids, that was actually a fairly efficient use of my time. Reading material aloud tends to be a family activity, and even the younger kids absorb a great deal although they don't always seem to be paying attention – things they say later on, or their familiarity with the material when we returned to it for 'their turn' proved this was sinking in.

Plus, I *like* to read to them, I had the *time* to read to them, and the family-time (even Dad enjoyed this when he was home – we school on weekends and on car-trips as well… because it's fun… for some of us anyways) was valuable.

But… it wasn't always enough to just *read* to them.

They really need(ed) to *do* things, *physical* things, and preferably *Real World* things to absorb and understand a topic. Some things are easier to make this happen for than others – for example Civic/History/ Geography (homeschooling doesn't have to draw sharp boundaries!) was well supported by their model government teams, participating in a couple of protests and get-out-the-vote phone banks, and even a trip to Washington D.C. (family vacation at the Smithsonian and Supreme Court!).

I use the word "supported" and not "supplemented" intentionally in this context.

These activities weren't "nice add-ons," they were absolutely core to the way these three kids of mine needed to have the information presented to them. (*Need*, I should say. Two of them are still homeschooling with me.)

Some things… are harder to make work like this.

Math is one of those areas.

My overly social, competitive kids appreciated having math teams/ competitions and a "Math Circle" to support their needs in that way. Math Circle (the concept comes from Soviet-era scientists and mathematicians who defected to the USA and set up less boring math learning environments for their own and their American colleagues' kids, based on the small group discussions that were all they were allowed in the USSR) gave us the opportunity to add in a variety of hands-on (if not real world) learning experiences, like discussing voting and cryptography and fractals... and mouse-trap catapults and Nerf guns (which got totally out of hand, but gave us a chance to talk about parabolas and quadratic equations so they could see who could shoot something the farthest).

But... I had to create and run Math Circle.

I did it because we had homeschooling friends who were scared of math and science, and homeschooling friends who were scared of math but loved science... but we needed to find (or grow) a group of other people that cared about Math once my oldest daughter got interested in it. I didn't want her excitement to be another Barbie fatality of our society's math-phobia (remember the talking Barbie in the early 80's that said "Math is hard, let's go shopping!" It was brief, apparently, Mattel killed that phrase quickly, but... there's a reason it ended up in a doll in the first place.)

We ran Math Circle for four years. It was a blast, and I loved it — and, honestly, that is where I learned to love math. To keep this thing going, we needed to have some sort of a presentation about some cool math topic every week... and while I recruited as many speakers as I could, I still ended up doing the bulk of them. I'd figured out I was *good* at math a couple years earlier... but hunting for interesting topics and figuring out how to present them to a group of kids *and adults* (including a former *Math professor* whose kids were involved, yikes!) was a huge challenge.

And it's super-hard to get other people excited about something if you aren't yourself, so...

...I had to learn to be excited.

I don't necessarily recommend going to this extreme, but a parent does what they have to do, right? (If any of you readers out there *do* decide to start a Math Circle, please check out the resources at the back of this book. And you can also email me. I have some very detailed lesson plans to help you get started.)

Math Circle ended before the pandemic... and a year or so before my oldest daughter went to college, none of the other kids being passionate enough to make me keep going with this.

But Kids 2, 3, and 4 are still audio-/hands-on-learners.

So, what now?

Well... we've tried a number of things. Khan Academy videos, and ProdigyGameOnline are helpful. So are things like building a shelter for our goats, 3D printing (and learning to use the CAD app to build their own stuff), an annual Balsa Bridge competition, and a variety of other such tools. Great Courses has some absolutely stellar video series on math from Arithmetic on up; the videos are oriented towards adults, so the tone is not at all condescending (kids pick up on condescension from teachers incredibly fast), and we were able to get some of them at our local library for free!

Competitions – which, I really do think are an entire Learning Style of their own, at least the way my kids do it – help me figure out where they are, and emphasize Problem-Solving and what I call "sideways thinking". As I said in Chapter One, we don't do enough Drill-and-Kill for our kids to be fast enough to be top competitors most of the time, but they seem to enjoy thinking about things differently – it gets them out of the rote memorization stuff. They do Math Kangaroo, which is K-12th; MathCounts, which is 6th-8th; and in the past have also done AMC 8/10/12 (kids can compete in a given one of them until they are past those grades). My oldest daughter still competes in college-level math competitions.

FIRST Lego League is not a Math competition, but they have to do an engineering research project and program a robot – and we are careful to draw the connections to the skills they have learned from math: sequential, logical thinking especially, but also data analysis and being able to critically read articles and websites for information. Science Fairs would be another way to get that sort of a connection.

We use Singapore Math (Primary Mathematics – Standards Edition) workbooks and they do just the reviews until they hit topics they aren't familiar with, and then I assign them to do Exercises from that previous section until they are ready to move on. This setup lets the kids have primary control over their math learning – they choose the when and where and bring the day's completed work to me to be checked. When there's an unfamiliar topic, I help them through it.

After the 6th grade Singapore books, we switch to Art of Problem-Solving, which is a "discovery-based" program...

Which, honestly, *doesn't really work that well* for my *audio-/hands-on-learners,* but we hit a different problem.

My oldest daughter used Art of Problem Solving... and she did fantastically... and the younger kids are determined that this is a great math program. I have tried to pry them loose at various times... but they also dislike change (even the teens) and don't want to "waste time" trying other programs when this one is right here.

Since they aren't *fighting* me about it... I respect their preferences and simply try to support them the best I can and suggest other resources (like Khan Academy videos) when they get stuck.

I have to mention Math-U-See for audio-/hands-on-learners, because several other homeschooling moms (whose kids weren't quite so stubborn) absolutely *swear* by it and told me it absolutely *had* to be in this book. One of these moms stated that it is the *ONLY* effective program for the hands-on-learner, and she is the type who looked at the options available exhaustively before settling on it.

Math-U-See has taken the idea of manipulatives – as many of us are familiar with from Montessori Early Childhood education (those Cuisinaire rods that show how 1's build into 10's, which build into 100's, and so on... I did similar demos with Legos and playdough for my kids) – and develops the manipulative approach to go through the upper grades, using videos along with the texts. The program goes up through High School Calculus.

Having not worked with Math-U-See myself, I can't say if the higher math stuff is good enough for the STEM-oriented kid who wants to be an engineer or scientist. (If you know a kid who used this program and went on to obtain a Bachelor's degree or higher in science or engineering, please let me know!)

What *has* been spectacularly successful for audio-learner Child #2, and seems to be working for audio-/hands-on-learner Child #3, is *dual-enrollment*.

Dual-enrollment is when a pre-college kid enrolls for a class at a college or university. I'm saying "pre-college kid" instead of "high schooler" or even "teen" because most universities are willing to accept younger local kids so long as they take the SAT or ACT and get a certain minimum score. The score needed to register for dual-enrollment is usually significantly lower than the lowest score the college will accept for "regular" students, but once they are in, they are taking the class just like the college students – same work, same deadlines, same exams. And the same *grades*. The college will give them a transcript, and the credits will be applicable to a college degree. The cost per credit-hour is sometimes quite a bit lower for dual-enrolled students as well.

Dual-enrollment can be an excellent option for covering those more advanced courses that you, the Homeschooling Parent, don't want to (or feel you can't). Community (2-year degree or "technical") colleges may offer classes down to Pre-Algebra or at even earlier levels.

TRUE STORY

One family of our acquaintance has their kids doing *all* their "High School" classes as dual-enrolled students. Their kids graduate with their High School diploma *and* Bachelor's degree simultaneously. And they have a great deal of control over their schedule – the kids are both performing artists, though they are getting degrees in math and science – which has been important for this family.

Other in-person options can include: those ubiquitous Kumon learning centers (but be aware that the Kumon focus is on Drill-and-Kill), Russian Schools of Math (somewhere between Math Circle and Drill-and-Kill, so there's rigor but also some variety), local tutors, and homeschool groups.

The Waldorf approach, which I mentioned earlier, introduces and develops Math skills through physical activities (the OakMeadow curriculum was developed out of Waldorf, but has wandered a bit far and I am not sure if they retain this component). Excellent resources for learning about this approach include the books by Donna Simmons (Christopherus Press); the books by Melisa Nielsen (A Journey Through Waldorf Homeschooling); and the books by Eric Fairman (Path of Discovery). I've used all of them, and found them all to be helpful.

Online curricula (do they work?)

They can. And as you look around for options, you'll get a great number of recommendations from other homeschoolers for online curricula. You'll be told that it's a great time-saver, because the kid just has to log in and you don't have to prep, grade, or work through it with them. You also get an outside (presumably less biased) evaluation of your child's skills.

For parents who need to work for pay (or with other children or have health care issues in the family that require time and attention) while their child homeschools, online curricula can be a huge blessing.

However, you should be aware before jumping into one that you still need to make sure your kid logs in, completes assignments (especially if they are time-dependent), and then acquire the transcripts in a form useful to you. You may also need to interact with teachers.

Keep in mind that online means on-screen – and if you, like me and so many of us – are trying to whittle screentime down to something reasonable, you have to think about that, too. If all the screentime you are okay with is used up "doing school" will there be any time left for play? Will limiting screentime-play because of "doing school" online get you into an ongoing battle with your kid?

You also want to keep an eye out for *how* the online course works. Going through a public-school-based online curriculum may not be your best choice (then again, it might be, so do your research and let me know about your experiences, both positive and negative). The NTI approaches that most school-districts in the USA put in place during the pandemic were an attempt to re-invent the wheel. There are reputable homeschool companies out there that have spent *decades* figuring out how to teach online effectively – it absolutely baffled me that the school-districts didn't just contract with these companies, or at least hire them on as consultants, but I haven't heard of that happening anywhere. The companies that are still in existence after ten or more years are probably in business because their product *works*. Don't saddle your kid – or yourself with some hack thrown together by overworked public school teachers because their district or state didn't pay for a product with history. Some districts and states are actively marketing their School-at-Home options now, and they make it ridiculously easy to sign up, but convenience isn't worth the lack of learning you'll be dealing with later... only you can say if the cost (or lack of cost) *is*.

And don't forget: *whichever* online curriculum you choose you can also *ditch*. Even partway through the year. (See if you have wiggle-room on government-/custody-mandated curricula – a judge or court-appointed advocate or other official may have the authority to agree with you that you need to switch. Or at least know how to make that happen.)

You might be getting the idea that I'm opposed to online curriculum – for math as well as other things. And I'm not, really.

But I'm wary.

I'm wary because my kids – especially the youngest three (10yo, 12yo, 15yo) all spend inordinate amounts of time on-screen already.

And I'm wary because study after study has shown reduced learning outcomes for online learning, for everyone from pre-schoolers through adults.

And the results from the pandemic years of NTI are still just coming in, but the early data suggest it's not pretty.

Especially for math.

My husband is an engineering professor at a large state university. Pre-pandemic, they only accepted students into the engineering program who had a good grasp of Calculus, making exceptions for kids from rural schools who didn't have access to Calculus classes. Those kids (with Pre-Calculus) would start a semester behind… but it wasn't right to deny them the opportunity.

The kids coming in post-pandemic are weak on *Pre*-Calculus.

Note that Calculus (not *Pre*-Calculus) is a prerequisite for *all* their other engineering courses. They can get some General Education requirements out of the way, but they can't seriously start working towards their engineering degree until they can pass Calculus. These are *paying* students, mind you – and they could be my kids or your kids.

And my husband's analyses of graduation and retention data in his engineering program show that passing Calculus is the biggest predictive factor in whether a person stays on to get their engineering degree. Taking loans to pay for an engineering or science degree is a good deal (and paying them back is eminently do-able)… so long as you get the degree.

It's not these kids' fault that they went through a pandemic and suffered through ill-conceived, poorly-implemented NTI. It's not the teachers' fault – they were working with what they had. And – like I said – it took *decades* for homeschooling curriculum companies to figure out how to teach well online. (I'm inclined to blame districts and states… but we all know there was a money crunch as well… we are where we are…)

Because of all this, my husband's hard-line on homeschooling has been that *our* kids have to complete the equivalent of at least one college semester (or one High School year) of Calculus before they finish 12th grade. This is partly because all of them so far are interested in STEM fields (except for the 10yo; she wants to find unicorns). But it's not just because they want to do engineering or science – it's so that they have the *option* to do engineering or science. So that *our* kids aren't stuck taking an extra year in college, or struggling and giving up on the dreams they maybe didn't even realize they had… because we weren't able to help them learn math.

If the best way to do that is online, we go with online.

But with the stakes this high, my inclination is to use online as a *supplement,* not as our main Math curriculum.

Here's some of what we *do* use from the multifarious and overwhelming array of online options:

1. We use ProdigyGameOnline semi-regularly – it is one of the 3-4 math activities my youngest two can do to "count for" doing math on a given day. Because we are trying not to encourage a vast amount of screentime, they are allowed to count it for "school purposes" at most once a week, although they can play it as a game (for fun, because they really do think it's fun) up to their usual screentime limits.

2. Khan Academy is more occasional. My High Schoolers use it when their books don't explain something well. I usually find out that they turned to Khan Academy some time later, in casual conversation. My current two High Schoolers are my top audio-/hands-on-learners, so it actually has surprised me that they don't go to Khan more often.

3. Great Courses – we used the *Fundamentals of Mathematics* series (on DVDs, so I'm not sure if this really counts) a few years ago when I was experimenting with different options. The youngest two (who were then 5 and 7) loved it and learned a great deal about fractions… they would actually ask me to put it on, and pause the video when a problem was put up to practice on. The middle two (my current High Schoolers) were 10 and 13yo and completely uninterested… but I may have just had the wrong set for them. We like the format, and have used Great Courses for other subjects. Again, another bonus is that many are available free from the library!

4. My older daughters (both in college) use a number of online resources, including just Zooming in to class when they are sick (or, ahem, sleepy) or watching the professor's pre-recorded videos. One of them took to watching a different professor's videos (same university) because he was better than the one teaching the class she was in.

I don't put down learning from TV/online but my conclusion so far has been that these media are great for getting someone *excited* about math (or other topics) or for exploring exotic fields that you wouldn't be able to find locally. My first sense that Math might be fun came in the 80's, watching *3-2-1 Contact* and *SquareOne TV* on PBS… but I didn't *learn* very much actual math from those sources, and my interest and enthusiasm was dried up and blown away by standard "Drill-and-Kill" type math classes both as a homeschooler (using the public school's curriculum, because there wasn't anything else my mom could find in those days) and in college.

It took needing to protect my oldest daughter's newborn love of math that made me really appreciate it.

Different amounts of parent-child interaction/input

Before you pick *any* curriculum for Math (or anything else) you should be aware of how much work the curriculum publisher is asking you to do. It would also be helpful to know if that goes down as you get more comfortable with the curriculum, and whether the schedules that are included with the curriculum are anywhere near do-able (or whether they will have you waking up in the middle of the night panicking because you are "behind").

The only real way to get answers to these is to try the thing – but asking around for the experiences of other people who have used the curriculum can get you started. Keep in mind that homeschool curriculum – and most especially *Math* homeschool curriculum is a very individualized experience.

For example, you may look at someone else's review and see that they – and you – have kids of similar ages, one of whom is on the ADHD spectrum, you both live in the suburbs, etc. But what the reviewer may not give detail on is that she was a math major in college and this is all easy for her. Or he might not mention is that they started using this curriculum just after they had a new baby, the kids' grandmother had passed away, and they moved.

I keep mentioning this sort of thing – even though I know you are reading reviews and looking for more than one review, and so on – because there is such a *wealth* of options out there. It's all too tempting to just give up and buy *something*.

How to Find the "Perfect" Homeschool Math Curriculum

1) Ask all your friends and online homeschool groups for recommendations

2) Research all the suggestions online until you cry.

3) "Rinse and repeat"

4) Go back and buy the first one you saw.

There are literally a zillion out there. Everything from Kitten Math (I kid you not) to Beast Academy (comic-book-style, for younger kids from Art of Problem Solving. My kids loved the comic-book textbooks and absolutely refused to have anything to do with the workbooks) to AOPS online to Calvert School to K12.

And, honestly, you cannot possibly compare every single homeschool math option out there against every other one and come up with some perfect ideal curriculum that will work the first time you take it out of the box and every time thereafter and your kids will universally adore. There are simply too many of them as you will see from this link: http://www.homeschoolmath.net/curriculum_reviews/

And it is ***TOTALLY FINE*** to just go ahead and buy something. A print curriculum, an online curriculum, an online class, an in-person class, a tutor's time.

If you need permission to just let go and do this: I hereby give you permission.

With 2 caveats:

1. You promise to buy the *smallest* amount of curriculum you can to try it out (Not a whole year, please… or even worse, a whole year for *all the subjects*).

2. You understand that if you hate it, or your kids hate it, you will give it a try of no less than 2 weeks, but you will not persist with something everyone hates for more than a month.

Your ideal curriculum should have as many of the following features as possible (re-rank them according to what matters most to you):

*   It is FLEXIBLE (The included schedule doesn't make you feel guilty, it has suggestions for activities to supplement OR leaves time for you to come up with occasional cool things)

*   It will allow your kid to meet the learning goals you (or you *with them*) have set. (Preferably short-term *and* long-term goals… at least in the sense that you're willing to switch it up for something else if it's not working)

*   It fits the learning style of the kid you are buying it for

*   It isn't a horrible fit for the next kid you might want to use it with (based on learning style)

*   It works with *your* teaching/learning style (not a lot of people talk about this, so you may have to read carefully to try to tell)

*   You can buy one book at a time. (This is one reason why I love Singapore. Child#1 was chugging along until she hit the

7th grade books and those were terrible - for her (it was a bad match between kid and curriculum). We could switch gears quickly to AOPS. Where I also buy one book at a time.)

- There is a used-curriculum market for this item (Are you finding listings on eBay or Craigslist? Does your local homeschool curriculum store resell this item?)

- The amount of your time it takes is worth it for the results you get.

And then there's the last one…

Cost

Ultimately, this is the often the kicker. And it's actually a big part of *why* I strongly encourage you to buy the tiniest bit of curriculum you can.

Not just the first time, either, when you're testing it out to see if it's going to work for you at all. But *every* time.

Yes, the bundled curriculum that has a year's worth of math (or a whole year's worth of *all subjects*) is cheaper than adding up all those pieces together. And if you are absotively posolutely sure you are going to *use* all those pieces, it's worth it.

Maybe I'm weird, but I am never that confident, especially about something that I probably ordered online and have never seen and touched. Heck, even if I bought it at a curriculum store or a homeschool convention, even if my kids and my husband were along with me and seemed to be totally bought into the new thing… I don't trust it. And I don't want to pay for a heap of pieces we never end up using rather than *one* or *two* items we don't end up using.

Often taking just one or two items that you don't end up using (or maybe don't even plan to use) will change the value of the bundle to you so that it's more cost-effective to buy just the parts you want.

Maybe I'm weird – maybe my kids and I are more finicky than the norm. But *every* single time I have gotten excited and bought a bundle (Royal Fireworks Press had this amazing 4th grade pack) – or all the parts (I went a little nuts with Singapore's extras a few years back) – I have ended up using…

…*none* of them.

I'm not blaming Royal Fireworks Press or Singapore, please note. I made my choices with open eyes. And *I* still think the RFP pack has amazing stuff in it, and that all the supplemental Singapore stuff would have helped my kids tremendously.

But my kids were not on-board with these plans. And the amount of energy it would have taken to make the family conform to my Vision of Our Homeschool… was just not worth it in the end.

Did the kids miss out on some valuable lessons? Sure they did.

Did they pick up – somewhere else – the things we didn't formally cover in another way? Yep, that, too.

The biggest argument, to my mind, for buying a homeschooling bundle, is that the re-sale value is higher because some other poor homeschooling parent will get stars in their eyes over having *all right there* and at *such a good price*.

We're all looking for deals… but we're all also willing to ante up a little cash (or a lot) for

A. Convenience

B. Confidence (someone put this together who knew what they were doing)

C. Compartmentalization (phew! It treats each subject separately, just like "real" school)

D. Calendar (someone else figured out your schedule for you)

Like the jewelry store ads say about diamonds, though, it all comes down to that all-important fifth C… Cost

You can homeschool – including teaching math – completely for free. There are books at the store (and in the library) to tell you how. I haven't tried to look at their recommendations for quality – and with Google around it's pretty easy to find options once someone tells you it's possible.

Free can be *very* high quality in homeschooling supplies. It can also be crappy.

Only you can decide if the first four Cs (and the reliance on someone else's idea of how to do things) are worth the Cost.

I spend less than three thousand dollars per year on homeschooling. (And could easily do it for less).

That is for homeschooling *four kids* – and it used to be about the same for *six*.

There have been a few exceptions: such as the year my oldest daughter was doing AP Chemistry and I forgot how much I don't like doing labwork and went a bit crazy and bought us a microscope and labware and kits for about seven AP Chemistry experiments. (Each one was separate… and we did 4-5 of them.)

I'm also not counting college tuition (our oldest two are in college). Or dual-enrollment – where we are it's about $100/credit hour for a dual-enrolled kid, and the average college course is 3-4 credit hours. At two classes per semester for one kid, that's $1200-$1600.

And I'm not counting the gymnastics teams my older daughters were on for eight years. If they'd been in school, I'm not sure if we'd have anted up for gymnastics… but I can't say we *wouldn't* have either, since most of the other team families were also public school families.

And… I'm not counting driving the kids around (mostly because I don't feel like doing the calculation). With six kids, we drive a 15-passenger gas-guzzler.

On the one hand, we don't have to participate (or pay into) fundraisers, we have choices about travel (and can do that when prices are better), there's no uniforms or dress-codes for extra shopping, and so on. On the other hand, we use more AC in the summer because we're home all day, and more food for the same reason.

Our biggest single expense is sending two kids to the model government teams – which are run by the YMCA and the fees cover costs. The next biggest thing is Lego team. These are optional items, and we chose them despite the cost because they add a huge amount of value to our homeschool.

Our *Math* expenses are about $200 for the year, most of which is registrations for competitions (MathCounts and Math Kangaroo), and some of it is for Singapore Math books, of which we are on the last set I will ever buy. My 10yo is about to start on the Art of Problem Solving books in the Spring, and those are not consumable workbooks; they are the kind of books where you keep a separate notebook and write in that, so the one Pre-Algebra book has now lasted through 6 kids.

Math doesn't spoil. It's infinitely re-usable.

We do use a few free add-ons, which I've already mentioned: ProdigyGameOnline, Khan Academy, and Math-Aids.com (to print off semi-customized worksheets in almost any math topic imaginable).

Math-Aids.com does offer a membership to get rid of the ads – for about $25/year, and I do that every now and then.

ProdigyGameOnline also has a membership option so the kids can do... *something* more... (not sure exactly what). My now-10yo tried it a few years ago and didn't ask to renew the paid membership, so it apparently wasn't a big deal to her. (At the time, it was about $40 annual, and down to about $20 with the group buys they make available. The FB groups doing the buys are happy to take more people in to meet the number they need.) My child's ProdigyGameOnline membership didn't give *me* any more options for my Teacher account, though, and since there are already a ton of options for me as the "teacher"... we let it go.

And there are tons of free math videos to stimulate your interest in fun topics from bottles that have no inside to hexaflexagons to... you name it.

Otherwise, it's paper, notebooks, pencils, pens... a set of compasses and protractors and straight-edges. We did buy the kids calculators, but they only use them for one section of MathCounts and for AP Physics, not for regular math.

If your budget is more tolerant than mine, the sky is the limit, of course. You can pay for individualized tutoring in every subject, including Math, and hire professionals to do it. You can send the kid for Math Camps and Math Workshops and...

... and if you were into all that stuff, you probably wouldn't be reading *this* book.

Just pick a nice, simple math curriculum that you can buy one book at a time for (Singapore books are about $20 per workbook at this writing). Sell off what you don't need. Use some of the online freebies when you need some extra goodies.

It'll be fine.

Chapter Three:

Math Circles
(going beyond curriculum,
making it cool)

- **What is a math circle?**
- **Other math communities for kids and families**

LIKE MOST HUMAN ACTIVITIES, MATH is often something better done in a community.

A community of people who are doing math provides a number of benefits, including the simple conviction that you aren't the only "weirdo" stuck doing it. If you happen to *love* math – or have a kid who does – that kind of validation is absolutely critical.

A big part of the story of how my oldest daughter decided to become a mathematician – from the viewpoint of the rest of our family, anyways – was Math Circle.

> **OUR STORY**
> As I've mentioned before, Child#1 was utterly gung-ho about dinosaurs until about age 12, then spent a couple years messing around with other ideas before

settling on Physics. At that point, she was beginning to *appreciate* math for its use as a tool for Physics, but her most direct interest in the subject itself was because of her highly competitive nature.

Our family had been attending a certain weekly playgroup for a few months, and she was by far the oldest child there. Her next-younger sister was the next-oldest child. We were really going for the sake of the younger four kids, and the girls had to come with because it was the only way I could get them to gymnastics practice on time. They played "Big Sister" to everyone, indulged their own less-mature sides with active play (we all need that!), or brought a book.

The kick-in-the-pants moment came when she discovered that a child nearly three years younger than her was at the same point in the math book that she'd been dawdling over (Art of Problem-Solving (AOPS) Introduction to Algebra, if you're wondering). At that point we didn't know this boy's mom was a former math teacher and his dad was a former math professor. We just knew that he was at the same place in the same book.

I thought it was interesting that they were using the same curriculum (AoPS was relatively unknown in my other homeschooling circles then), but my oldest daughter's reaction was... about what I have come to expect from my kids. She was not going to *let that boy beat her!* Having the next-younger sibling nipping at their heels academically has motivated more than one of my kids to get a move on... but at that point in time, my oldest daughter was far ahead of her sister, and there had been no "upwards pressure" until then.

So, my "give it all you got" girl threw herself

into finishing her book. She made me sign her up for MathCounts – it was her eighth grade year and hence her last chance – and then proceeded to *flatten* the competition at our chapter meet. (She spooked when we went to State… but those things happen.)

And… then we hit a wall.

We knew plenty of kids (and parents) who thought we were *weird* for liking science.

We knew a handful of kids (and parents) who liked science – but they still seemed to think math was *hard*. And *unpleasant*. And…

Peer pressure is a Thing, folks.

I could see where this was going.

My oldest daughter was going to cave and decide to be interested in something that she could share the joy of with at least *some* of her friends. Just as close to *90%* of girls do in Middle School. The statistics show that boys and girls are mostly pretty excited about math and science up until that age, and then *both* genders start to "lose interest" (or be discouraged from pursuing that interest). It's *both genders*… but girls drop off from an interest in STEM fields, especially the Physical Sciences (Physics, Chemistry, Engineering) at a much higher rate.

These "choices" have real-world consequences. Girls without STEM-skills grow up into women without STEM-jobs. And STEM-jobs *pay a great deal more.* If you want your daughter (or son) to be able to support themselves as an adult (and be in a position to help you when you're older) and they have an early interest in STEM – please, encourage it!

(*That's why I'm reading this book, you say.* I know, I know.)

Let me be specific here. These were kids from the *homeschooling* community I am talking about – people whose moms and dads took an active interest in their daily learning and sought out activities to encourage their interests on a regular basis. Our public school friends (whose parents had to fit such things around a school schedule) were even less enthusiastic about math. And my professor-husband's colleagues' kids were all adults.

Now. I was in my early 40s by this time. I'd gotten over (finally) my belief that I "wasn't good" at math – my mother blamed that belief on my kindergarten and first grade years in public school until the day she died, but I can't say so with certainty.

But I still didn't like math *for its own thing*.

However, my daughter did and what does a homeschool mom do? Support her kids' interests, of course?

Google and Facebook quickly made it obvious that there weren't any great options around for us in regards to a participating in a community of people who enjoyed Math for itself (later on I found the Russion School of Math in Louisville… but that was later).

But… the friend who – several years earlier, and had by then moved away – had first told me about Art of Problem Solving and MathCounts (and model government… we owe her a great debt) had also tossed out the idea of a "Math Circle".

What is a math circle?

The idea of Math Circles was brought to the USA by the highly qualified Soviet-era scientists and mathematicians and engineers who sought asylum here during the Cold War. In the Soviet Union they had been forbidden to meet in groups of more than a handful of adults – to try to prevent them from using their big brains to spread sedition.

What can you do with a scant handful of people? Well, one thing is chess, and that is part of why there are so many great Russian (and former-Soviet citizen) chessplayers.

But another thing is *math*. Which really does get more interesting when you can discuss it with other people (not do drills together, *play* with it). And if you make family-and-friends Game Night into Math Night (because you don't have access to Monopoly and Hungry, Hungry Hippos… because you're in the Soviet Union) and bring the *kids* into it… now you might have enough people to make it *really* interesting.

Of course, kids don't *know* a lot of math to start… but they can ask some really interesting questions…

And in math – and science – getting into the habit of asking interesting questions and then playing around with ideas while you think about answers is key to going very far. It's making the whole enterprise *playful*.

Well, then these highly skilled mathematicians and scientists and engineers came to the USA and discovered that Freedom from Oppression… didn't translate to a particularly stellar math experience for their kids in school. And they were re-forming their little "Math Circles" with their colleagues at companies and colleges, because it was fun and they missed the social aspects… so…

The US Math Circle movement was born. You can read up about it at https://mathcircles.org . They have a number of fine publications as well as great online resources.

So, what *is* a "Math Circle"?

I'm going to compare it to a knitting circle or a sewing circle. It's less a *club*, and less a *class*, and more a group of friends of all ages who get together to talk about math.

Boring City for those of us non-math-y people, right?

Well... it doesn't have to be, but

1. It's hard to get anyone who isn't "into" math to even show up and give it a try – disdain or intimidation, take your pick, they don't come; and

2. You have to keep an open mind about math when you do show up and... *man*, is that hard!

But it is an *absolutely invaluable* social resource for anyone trying to *learn* to like math, or trying to support someone else who already does.

I credit the Louisville Area Math Circle – which I created and ran for four years, taking a break for Summer – for helping my oldest daughter keep her love of math alive as she moved forwards. We probably *could* have sent her off right from the start (at age 14) to take college classes in math, join the university Math Club (which she *did* do once she started taking college classes at 17), and let her find her community that way. Given who she is, that might have worked well – she is an incredibly confident young woman, and was an incredibly confident girl. I suppose that once you've stared Death in the eye and laughed at it by throwing yourself into back handsprings on a beam, mere human scorn is a frail thing. (Yes, I'm a nerd who is pro-sports. Not pro-"being a sports mom" – that sucked, for all that it was great for the kids – but pro-sports because my daughters got so much out of challenging themselves that way.)

I'm not sure that being thrown headfirst into college classes would work for every young math lover out there, however. And Math Circle was a good bridge in that gap.

It *also* did great things for my younger five kids (or at least the three of them who remember it).

None of them love math.

A *couple* of them can appreciate elegance or beauty in math.

Most of them *hate* it, at least part of the time.

All of them can see how to use it as a tool and know that it is a tool in *their* toolkit.

All of them had a chance to see how math can be *fun*… and actually *had* fun doing math.

How?

Well, the "typical" Math Circle seems to rise out of a need perceived by math professors (often of Russian/former-Soviet-citizen descent). They find the space, the time, then recruit some parents in the community… and begin to grow a program. These Math Circles are often aimed at kids… and out of deference to the fear and aversion of us non-math-y people (and working with the way kids are used to learning in school), some of these do edge over into something closer to a class, as best I can tell.

Our Louisville Area Math Circle was a little different.

First, it was a *parent-driven* initiative, and we didn't get a great deal of involvement from a university – although University of Louisville did allow us meeting space, though my husband.

Second, I tried to keep it as close to either a "seminar" (with guest speakers) or a hands-on learning experience as I could. By contacting the University of Louisville Math Department I ended up with a graduate student and a couple of undergraduates who came in and took turns explaining interesting things to everyone, like Cryptography (code-breaking – how cool is that!) and "learning math like the Ancient Greeks" (meaning geometry with only a straight edge and compass).

One of the local math professors is a national expert on Voting Theory (as in, he gets interviewed on broadcast networks to explain it) and since we started in 2016, this was perfect! It got even better when he casually mentioned that he had homeschooled his own kids. We followed up his talk on Voting Theory with a couple of weeks of counting beans and learning about the problems in "bean-counting" (accurately keeping track of large numbers).

As I mentioned before, we also made Mouse-trap catapults and competed to see who could shoot farther. It let me bring in some Physics, talking about angles and parabolas and quadratic equations. Did all the kids know what everything was about? Certainly not – we had kids ranging from age 2 to 16 and a slew of adults of varying backgrounds. But it was a *memorable* experience for the older ones (and the adults). Even my child who was all of 9 years old at the time remembers enough to have a healthy appreciation for – and *interest in* learning about parabolas and quadratic equations (and it likely fed his interest in archery, as well).

We did stuff with fractals, including coloring in triangle fractals and adding our pictures together on the floor to make a gigantic one.

We solved math puzzles… and left them behind – unsolved – on the whiteboards for the college students who also used the building. We told math jokes. ("An infinite number of mathematicians walk into a bar. The first one orders a glass of water. The second one orders half a glass of water. The third one orders a quarter-glass. After the fourth one orders an eighth of a glass, the bartender shakes his head, fills up two glasses and served all infinity of them." Yeah, it works… and we did a demo with water in plastic cups to see. Some of those cups were still hanging around my house until last week!)

A third component of the Louisville Area Math Circle was our Math Team. This part was just for kids, and no one had to participate in team in order to enjoy Math Circle. The team was run by the former math professor dad of the boy who had "inspired" my oldest daughter – his kids and mine are still close friends, and that boy is also getting his degree in Mathematics.

The kids prepped together – but competed as individuals, even for MathCounts, which has Team Rounds. They competed in MathCounts, AMC (American Mathematics Competition) 8, AMC 10, and AMC 12. (I discovered the Math Kangaroo competition later on – it includes levels from K-12 and was a more comfortable fit for my younger kids.)

I ended up teaching about half the topics – which meant *learning* about those topics in advance and sufficiently well to be able to explain them.

If that sounds scary and overwhelming… well, yes, thank you for noticing. It was.

HOWEVER, if you are using a bought curriculum for math, you essentially are doing the same thing all week long every week. Or – if your kid is doing online classes – you're trying to untangle them after someone else tangled them up… and having to learn it all then.

By running Math Circle – and teaching/leading – half the topics I had *control* over what those topics were and how we would do it. I picked up a couple of *really great* popular math books at the bookstore (*Coincidences, Chaos, and All That Math Jazz* by Burger and Starbird; and *Things to Make and Do in the Fourth Dimension* by Parker) and sometimes did a little bit of Googling if I needed to understand something else. I knew that if *I* were bored with what we were doing, the kids would be, too.

I had to *get over myself and my dislike of math* … which was good for me.

And I had to get a lot more confident, since there was that dad sitting in the audience who likely knew the topic better than I did (the math team coach). And there were the older kids, who *loved* knowing something I didn't, or catching me in an error (didn't we all at that age?). And I was trying to engage and entertain everyone from my 4-year-old daughter to my 16-year-old daughter… to other people's less-forgiving kids in all the ages between.

It was totally worth it.

Even if my oldest daughter – and that boy whom she felt competitive with – had decided math was *not* the be-all and end-all of their existence, it would have been worth it.

I learned to actually *like* something that I had hated, feared, and then just avoided.

I still don't particularly like doing taxes, but working out a budget, or comparing prices isn't as scary as it was.

Homeschooling isn't just for the kids, folks.

It's for *us, too.*

Other math communities for kids and families

Okay, let's assume there isn't a Math Circle near you, and you're not insane enough to try to start a whole new organization.

What are your options to find communities where there is enough of an appreciation for math that your kid (and, ideally, you and the rest of your family) will feel supported?

We've covered most of them by now, here and there, but I'm going to list all the things I can think of here, so they're easy to find:

- Russian School of Mathematics. There are Russian Schools of Math all over the USA – it's actually a franchise, I think. They focus on *kids,* and it's a *classroom* situation. There is a constant challenge... which can be a good thing. They try to build community with their member families and they work to get kids to think about different aspects of math. The Russian School in Louisville has been wonderful to us, allowing my kids to participate (pre-pandemic, we've been online since) in Math Kangaroo at their facility. They tell me they have families coming from as far as St. Louis! (Which is over four hours of driving.)

  It wasn't the right fit for my family – partly due to cost (six kids!), partly due to conflicts (gymnastics, anyone?), and partly because what they are trying to create – a Math Positive Environment – in a couple hours a week is what my family was *living* by the time we discovered the Russian School. (More on that coming up.)

- Math Clubs. Pretty much every university or college will have one – my oldest daughter belonged to the Math Club at University of Louisville and now runs the Math Club at Purdue. Most universities allow "community members' to participate in many clubs... and dual-enrolled kids are college students and can definitely join.

High schools, or even middle schools, may have them as well. You could support an overworked, but enthusiastic teacher in getting one started if school-rules will allow your kid to participate. (If not, perhaps you can work it out with the teacher to do this outside of school and off-campus. Many teachers are dying to do things like this, but can't handle it alone. And many of them have their hands tied by state or district policies regarding homeschoolers, even if their principal is agreeable.)

- College classes. At a 4-year university, your kid will probably find like-minded souls right in class, if they are willing to speak up and talk to the other students (or the professor). Try to avoid the big classes that all the first-year engineering students are taking in math – those are often designed as weed-out classes and unless your kid loves a challenge, *loves* math, and is slightly a masochist, it's not going to be an ideal fit. Have them try the classes meant for math majors – those students are there because they want to be.

At a 2-year technical college you get more of a mix: a lot of non-traditional (aka "returning" or "adult") students who are trying to build a career while raising a family and may not have time to socialize, even if they are excited about math. You also get young adults who aren't sure of what they want to do and are diddling around (my brother-in-law was a bit of both after the Navy... he got himself together, but only *after* spending a year skipping math classes). And you get some who are there for the pure love of the subject.

One big *advantage* of 2-year colleges that I haven't mentioned yet is that it is likely to be easier to make it a parent-and-kid activity if you're minded to try. Take the class with your kid – which may make it more comfortable if your kid is on the younger/smaller side – and you each have a built-in study partner. Additionally, your kid gets to see that you are living what you preach. (Make sure you don't moan and groan too much… unless you don't mind them learning that's okay to do.)

TRUE STORY

Calculus is NOT like riding a bike. Nor is Linear Algebra.

When my oldest daughter was starting eleventh grade, my husband decided to do one of the (free, online) MIT OpenCourseware classes with her. They decided to do Linear Algebra – which I had covered many moons ago when I was a wee little undergrad myself. I got an A, and I had more confidence about Linear Algebra than other math even way back then.

So… piece of cake, right?

Um, no.

Of course, it would have been helpful if I had *done the homeworks* instead of just assuming that "refreshing my memory" by watching the lectures and then reading the book would be sufficient.

I kind of gave up trying after staring blankly at the first problem on the first exam (it's all self-paced, and the exams and solutions are online to print)… but I kept watching the lectures and I *did* learn a lot anyways (just conceptual, not useful without some more effort). The professor was absolutely *wonderful* to listen to – someone who

really *loved* his subject, and made you love it by contagion.

The next semester I watched Multivariable Calculus with them... but with reduced expectations for myself (I didn't try the exams, since I didn't want to put the effort in with the homework). It was another enthusiastic professor, so it was great to watch.

It was a great, family experience (our second daughter watched, too, but was with me on how much she could actually *do*... though now she's taking those classes in college as a Computer Science major, so it looks like she picked up the excitement, rather than being discouraged).

Well worth it to support my oldest daughter – and watch people talk happily about what they love!

- Chess Clubs. (Also, clubs that play Go.) There is heavy overlap between the community you would find interested in a Math Circle and people who play chess and Go. It's not a complete overlap, however, and since the focus is on chess, not math, you might or might not actually find the math people. (Try wearing T-shirts with math-jokes on them... the ones who gravitate to you are the math people.)

- Other Gaming clubs/groups. Probably not. Nerds and Geeks overlap a great deal, but tend to compartmentalize those areas of life, possibly because if you start "nerding out" at a Dungeons & Dragons game it may go super-well... or super-poorly and no one really wants to test that. Same for other fan organizations, like Trekkies or Star Wars or comic-book fans. On the other hand, they may *appreciate* that your kid likes math, even if they don't themselves. A pale substitute, but any water in the desert…

- Kids' Groups like Scouts (of various sorts), church groups, 4-H, and so on. These groups are often looking for someone willing to give a talk to the kids. One talk – an hour or two, cookies and juice are often involved. It's not a big time commitment, so you can try to find a math teacher or university professor (or some of the kids from the university Math Club) to give the talk. Remind them to have a hands-on activity.

- The downside of this one is that the depth is always going to stay a little shallow. But if your kid sees that there is even *one other kid* who is excited about math… and can keep in touch with them… it might be worth it. The history of math is rife with stories just like that – where one pair of kids supported each others' interests. And your efforts to bring a one-time math activity to your Scouting group might save *that* kid's enthusiasm as well as your own.

> **TRUE STORY**
> When my oldest daughter was a baby, we lived in Family Housing at the University of Michigan. A few days after my second daughter was born, one of the other moms from around our courtyard (a law student) came over with her 6-year-old daughter to see the new baby. While we chatted, it came up that her husband (a medical doctor in the Army) had taken over their 8-year-old son's birthday party and was teaching all the little boys to use Pythagoras' Theorem to solve triangles. (You remember – that's the a-squared plus b-squared equals c-squared thing.)

My friend said, with rolled eyes, that the boys were having a blast.

Part of that was surely the math, and the way this dad was presenting it. Eight-year-olds love to solve puzzles, and if you add "who can do this faster?" component you can be golden. *I* would never have thought of this for a party activity (and, despite hearing about this so early on) we've actually had almost no math involved in birthday parties for any of our kids.

But undoubtedly, what was really getting those little boys going was the *intense* and *enthusiastic* participation of an adult in *something they were doing.* Kids need social time with other kids, for sure, but for most of them, time with adults is what they get less of and really crave.

Summary: look for a community with a Math Positive Environment for your kid – and your family. Join one if you can, build one if you must!

Chapter Four:

Getting yourself on-board (Math for Moms and Dads [and other family members])

- **Playing solitary math games**
- **Seeing math in regular life**

S O A THEME YOU MAY have been seeing as we go is that *You the Parent* needs to get on-board with caring about math. (It helps if it's you, your co-parent, and any other important adults in your kids' lives as well.)

What does this mean?

It means:

- Being ready to engage with your kid over math when opportunities arise
- Showing your kid that *you feel* that math is FUN/beautiful/ useful
- Not allowing anyone to dis your child's interest in math (because they aren't good enough, because "that's just for nerds", or whatever pops out of people's mouths... kids *or* adults!)

- Never implying to your kid that there are bad things about math (that it's scary or hard) ... but rather working to transform your kid's negative associations to positive ones ("it's *challenging*, but we're tougher")

- Finding ways to bring math into your regular daily life together so it becomes "just another normal part of life"

- Finding ways to *play* with math together, because, hey, *FUN*

And all of this really comes down to ONE BIG THING:

- ***YOU MUST GIVE UP YOUR OWN AVERSION TO MATH.***

I'm not saying it's easy, people. It took me 15-35 years (depending on how you're counting) to give up my ***FEAR*** of math... and another 3 to go beyond that and reach the point where I could really try to be what my oldest daughter needed me to be as her support in loving and learning math.

But it wasn't just for her.

Not even mostly for her benefit.

It was for:

- My other five kids, who do NOT love math, but for whom I could show them a path to caring enough to *do* math.

- And it was for *me,* because I have enough other fears (large dogs, falling off of places, going at high speeds... spiders and snakes...) I didn't need *MATH* to be a fear, too!

  (And, OMG, but when Child #2 wanted to be an entomologist and now Child #5 wants to study snakes... I will TOTALLY take the kid who wants MATH...!)

But, we all know that Fear leads to Anger... and so on...

No, I don't think you need to worry about yourself or your kids turning to the Dark Side because you dislike Math. But do you really want a bunch of numbers and symbols lying on a page to determine what *you* will or won't do? And do you really want to go through all that Suffering?

Not worth Fearing or Hating Math. Really.

So, how exactly do you do this?

This chapter is about YOU, and how to start working on changing YOUR attitudes, so you can be the supportive parent we all dream of being. (Even for the kids who want to show you insects and snakes... or math puzzles.)

As with any fear or aversion that you are trying to defeat, the answer is desensitization – gradually exposing yourself to the thing or the idea a bit more each time until you aren't freaked out anymore. If being in the same room with a math book (or a kid doing math) makes you hyperventilate – then get a tutor for the kid and see if you can listen in from the next room... and move your chair a little closer, until you're right there with them. (Plenty of high schoolers need volunteer hours to graduate – tutoring a kid can sometimes count – call your local High School or ask around online for homeschooled teens. If your budget is a little more expansive, offer to pay.)

But you don't have to start with *Real* math to begin getting past your fear.

Just like with the kids, make it fun.

And because none of us like admitting to the kid (or anyone) how much we fear or dislike something... It can be easier to start by doing this on your own.

If you need the accountability of someone else making sure you *will* keep taking another baby-step forwards... find another math-averse parent. You can both do your thing and check in with each other, just like an exercise buddy. Or you can take your baby-steps together, if that works out.

I do *not* recommend you try to work on de-sensitizing yourself to math (or anything else) *with* your kid. That is even – or perhaps *especially* – if the kid is already math-averse. While a couple of grown-ups can laugh together awkwardly over a fear, or egg each other on, or sympathize, or at least *not take it personally* when we lose it… that's not true for kids. Especially our *own* kids or kids whom we have a close mentoring or teaching or family relationship who (technically) belong to others. Kids take *everything* their adult-mentors do personally (and when they start not to, they tend to go too far the other way and disregard *everything* we say or do… don't start down that path any earlier than you need to!).

You are much more likely to *reinforce* your kid's aversion to math if they see you struggling terribly with the emotional aspects.

Now, by contrast, if they see you struggling with the *concepts* or to do a particular *problem,* but you manage to keep a positive attitude? *That* teaches them a whole lot of positive life lessons about *grit* and *optimism* and *strength* and, oh, all those good things we want them to learn that have little to do directly with math.

So… start on your own, or with an adult friend.

And start by…

Playing solitary math games

Try Sudoku. It's not math, even though it uses numbers. It's pattern-recognition (which, okay… *fine*). You can get Sudoku games made with birds or animals – we have a lovely wooden set with colored glass 'jewels' that is pretty to look at and have out all on its own (plus it makes visitors think you're very intellectual).

If Sudoku doesn't float your boat (I was briefly obsessed, then wore myself out, and my sister-in-law who loves crossword puzzles refuses to even try), then here are some other options:

- Remember the Alphabet Game? You try to find the whole alphabet in sequence while driving somewhere? Great way to keep the kids occupied (though they can start fights over that, too, sigh…)

Try the NUMBERS GAME. Look for consecutive numbers as you drive.

This one can go on (literally) forever. Practically, it's awfully hard to find numbers in the triple-digits. (You can find a 1 as 1 or as part of 12 or 21 or 123 or 3012… but finding 123 takes a while!)

- Try the COUNTING GAME – just try counting anything that there are a reasonably large number of around you. Birds sitting on a wire, windows on a skyscraper, kids' toys left out on the fl– (on second thought, don't do that last. It'll add to the anxiety.)

- A more advanced variation would be the MULTIPLICATION GAME – the same thing, but stick to rectangular grids, like skyscraper windows or the tiles on the floor/ceiling of a doctor's office. Count horizontally and vertically and multiply them together. Do it in your head if you can, but it is perfectly fine for beginners to "cheat" and pull out the calculator on your phone or a piece of paper and a pencil.

(Want to make it more exotic? Try to figure out how many rooms are inside that skyscraper if it was all made up of rooms the same size, with no stairs or anything… how? Count the horizontal windows on a side that's at right angles to the side you already counted, and multiply that in with the number of windows you already did.)

- SOLITAIRE with cards on the computer is even a good way to get your brain going if just seeing numbers makes you queasy. Minesweeper (the old game from the 80's) is even better, because you have to reason things out and that uses the same parts of your brain as math.

Once you are comfortable with Numbers, you can try some other Math games. I don't, personally, really like math puzzles – in my not-so-humble opinion they are usually either thinly disguised word-problems or er else require some clever trick that I can rarely figure out. If liking math meant having to like math puzzles, I'd have given up ages ago –

after turning into a T-Rex and growling all over the house. (I'm actually not big into jigsaw puzzles either… so maybe this is just me.)

Any game that nudges you to think *logically* and *sequentially* is helpful at this stage.

Everyone is going to jump at the idea of Chess (which works as an individual game, since there are lots of free chess-apps), but Chess is intimidating all on its own for a lot of us, so I wouldn't go there.

The *idea* of getting an app to play against, though, that is a *brilliant* way to test yourself against your current level of aversion without having to let anyone else see. There are apps out there for zillions of games, including Othello, Yahtzee, Backgammon, and other things that we think of more as social games (more on those in the next chapter). I keep getting ads when I use DuoLingo (the language-learning app) for various logic-puzzles including filling bottles with colored liquids, mazes, and "save the trapped whatever" by pulling the levers in the right order things – they're just captivating enough that I watch the ads. (Logic puzzles where all the pieces are out there in front don't seem to bother me, LOL).

Go ahead and Google "single player math games" – most of what comes up is for kids (or cards), and there are some surprisingly lame games put out there for kids, so you'll have to triage. Don't waste your time on things that bore you or make you cringe. But give anything else a go.

My oldest daughter may have some better suggestions… she's been funneling such things down to the younger siblings for awhile now! (We'll be posting a list on https://www.RisingDragonBooks.com (just look for the Math button… we'll have it in January 2024) or you can email me at RisingDragonBooks@gmail.com for the most recent version.)

So, what's next after you can tolerate the idea of numbers and arithmetic?

Seeing math in regular life

If you've complained about – or listened to complaints about – "why do we have to learn Algebra? I'm never going to need this *in real life*" (let alone Geometry, Pre-Calculus, and so on) …well, you (or whomever was complaining) is mostly right.

In everyday living, there aren't a great many reasons to use those other things. They *do* pop up unexpectedly here or there, and when you least expect it, of course, but you can usually pawn those situations off on someone else whose math skills are a little less rusty if they scare you.

The main reason – for those who *don't* end up in STEM fields (which includes me now, as well) – is that Algebra and the other things teach a particular method of problem-solving that is incredibly useful *in everyday life.* The keys are *logic* and *sequential* approach and *knowing what's in your toolkit.*

If you learned how to sew a long, long, long time ago, and then your suddenly thirty and your toddler needs you to sew an eye back on their favorite stuffed animal, and you go digging for your needle and thread… it's going to be grisly. Do you even have a needle and thread anymore? Do you remember how to use them? And your kid is screaming the whole time in excruciating, emotional pain… *not helping,* kid!

Or your eight-year-old has a sudden deep-seated urge to bake cupcakes for your homeschool co-op. And, no, a box-mix (or the bakery) *will not do.* You have all the stuff – probably – because you *used* to bake occasionally (back in BC, Before Children).

Where do you even begin?

Well, you organize your supplies (what you can find), and determine if you have what you need or if a trip to the store (or putting this off a day, if that's feasible) is necessary. Cutie-poo's eye may be harder to put off, or the co-op may be meeting early tomorrow morning (yet another reason never to schedule anything before noon!) so sometimes we need to be creative.

How creative can we be?

If you were particularly good at sewing or baking when you *used to do it* you will have more skills at solving this problem now. No thread? Maybe you can get a few threads off that ravelly old blanket (not their lovey, one of yours). No eggs? What does the internet (or your cookbook, or your mom who's a thousand miles away) say about substitutes?

If you never learned those skills in the first place, it's harder to solve a new, unique situation.

If you learned *MATH,* you (hopefully) learned the *pattern* of skills needed to approach a unique situation and solve it, *even if it's outside your area of comfort or expertise.* As well as the *confidence* that you can do that.

And that, people, in a nutshell, is why you want your kids to learn about math and not be scared of it.

Back to you.

Once you begin to see where the Math is in your everyday life, it will make everything easier. For you as well as for helping your kids with math.

Where is the math in your everyday life? There are actual books that have been written to help teach your kids using "Consumer Math" or "Kitchen Table Math". Those will have more resources for you, and you can also use those as Google search terms. (Add the words "homeschool curriculum" and you'll get a ton.)

But we're looking at *you,* not the kids yet.

So, here's what *I* do. Besides the usual sorts of things we all get stuck with, like our grocery bills.

First, you need to know that we live on what would be a hobby farm (if any of us actually made a hobby of gardening… this is why we have goats) about an hour's drive away from… Well, from pretty much anything we want to do. So, we spend a *lot* of time in the car. I mean *a lot.*

And if there is anything more boring than driving a pack of kids around… it's driving them around for a minimum of two hours every time we leave the house. We've tried audiobooks, car-games, and more. Once we've had a kid-driver it's gotten better (from my perspective) because I can read – either aloud to them (yep, we car-school in addition to reading fiction) or to myself. And then there's the bickering…

Eventually we all default to silence – with or without the radio – and I resort to keeping myself from falling asleep doing things like this:

I started doing this one because I grew up with cars that had PROBLEMS and would burn oil or leak gas – and our first sign of a problem was that the gas mileage would be off. And then there was the time when I thought I had ten more miles to get to a gas station and ended up having to call a friend to rescue me.

So, what do I *do?* I calculate the miles per gallon of our last tank in my head. (This made a great lesson for the kids once I got comfortable doing it myself.)

A. I start out by assuming we went one mile per gallon, using the number of gallons that I put in the last time I filled the car – that's the number of gallons we used for the number of miles we traveled. We put 25-29 gallons in our van at once.

B. The result is pretty ugly (*one* mile per gallon – we couldn't afford to go anywhere! Even if there were anywhere close enough to go!). And it doesn't anywhere near match the actual number of miles we traveled, so I move on to 10 miles per gallon, which is easy to do in my head. (250 miles if we put in 25 gallons… but we probably went about 412 miles)

C. It's still incredibly *wrong* (our vehicles get ~16mpg on the van and ~39mpg on the car) …so then I try 20 miles per gallon (which is just doubling the last number). For the van, I'm now too far ahead when I compare the number of miles at 20mpg and the number we actually traveled. (Now I have 500 miles, which is 500-412=88 miles too many.)

So I try looking at 5 miles per gallon (125 in my example) and then adding that to the 10 miles per gallon number. That gives me the number of miles for 15mpg (125+250 =375). I subtract that number from the number of miles we actually traveled… and then I have a small number of miles left (usually between 25 and 50… in our example 412-375=37).

D. I can add the number of gallons we just filled (25) to find how many miles we would have traveled if we got 16mpg (375+25 = 400).

E. That number is still a little low, so I can decide to keep going to get more accurate, or I can decide that I'm happy we don't have weirdo stuff happening (like a gas-leak or burning oil). If I wanted to go on, I'd add half the number of gallons (12.5) that I'd filled to get 412.5… which is pretty darned close.

(I'm just adding, subtracting, doubling and halving – nothing too exotic.)

After doing this a couple times, I realized that the "mileage" that the car's computer was telling me was off – sometimes REALLY FAR off.

So… I might be saving us from dying on the side of the road when we run out of gas – it happened to a mom on a bridge I drive regularly.

I might be discovering whether the car needs maintenance.

I am definitely keeping myself occupied and awake!

Does calculating your car's fuel efficiency in your head not float your boat? Probably not. I know I'm a little weird. (If I'm *really* bored with listening to the kids bicker and we haven't filled the tank recently, I calculate how many gallons are in our swimming pool. Which you'd think I'd remember... but I don't, and since I can only remember a handful of unit-conversions while I'm driving... it keeps me occupied. [In case anyone is also weird and interested, I know how deep the pool is and how wide in feet; I can convert feet to inches and inches to centimeters; then centimeters to cubic centimeters to liters; then liters to kilograms to pounds; then pounds to gallons. Yes, I know there are much easier ways...])

Some more *interesting* ways to play with math in your everyday life could include:

- Fantasizing about your dream vacation (or home or car or kitchen re-model). Focus on the fun parts of it – like how much space that amazing stove would take up in your re-designed kitchen, or the cc's in that car's engine (or it's kWh capacity). Do NOT focus on the $$ values associated with your dream... unless you are actively able to work towards your dream. The goal here is to enjoy the numbers in terms of something you love.

- Check the accuracy of your speedometer (or odometer) while driving on the highway. Note the time as you pass a mile-marker and then the time when you pass the one for the next mile (in the USA there are likely interim markers at 1/10 or 1/8 mile... use those for extra fun!). If you were traveling at 60miles per hour, it should have taken you a minute to travel that distance. If you have a "co-pilot" with you, they can do a more accurate read on the time, but even just glancing at your car-clock should tell you if you were close to the right speed. (If you were traveling at 55mph, it should be a little longer than a minute [1:05], and if you were at 65mph, it should be slightly less [0:55]. [And if you were traveling at 80mph, 45 seconds, but I hope you were in Texas or Montana...])

- You can check the accuracy of your odometer even more easily (though I suggest you look at your trip odometer, since it measures in tenths of a mile, not just whole miles). Match it up to a mile-marker along the road, and compare.

- Order pizza for the family – or a party – and have fun with comparing numbers of slices to number of people. (Of course, then everyone has topping preferences… you can get a surprising amount of math-time with pizza!)

- Do what my family does with cake and divide it up evenly into the number of people present… has to be evenly or someone will cry foul! The kids breathed a sigh of relief when their older sister went back to college in August – dividing things evenly into 7ths is hard! (But oh, so good for them. And to quote Mr. Food – the television chef from the 70's and 80s who came from my hometown of Schenectady, NY – the cake was "ooh, it's so good!")

- Design a garden plot (or a windowbox – take it at your own pace – and pay attention to the spacing recommended on those seed packets and plant pots. How many extra seeds do you have?

- Plan a really cool Halloween costume that will require some sewing (maybe not a lot – like a cloak) or a tree-skirt for Christmas, table-runner for Halloween… something fun for a holiday you love. (Or for one you don't really love, so you haven't overscheduled it already!) Then calculate how much fabric you'll need. Fabric or paper-based crafts that involve cutting are particularly math-y, since you have to pay attention to having enough even after you trim corners and edges or make weird shapes. (By contrast, you can roll out cookie-dough or a pie-crust after combining the scraps and "cheat".)

- And don't forget letting your perfectionist side play a bit and match stripes at edges…

- And speaking of cookies… are you a "roll it out and cut as many of the same shapes out as possible" person? Or a "roll it out and assemble *all* your cookie cutters out and fit them on the dough as snugly as possible" person? I was shocked – *shocked*, I tell you – when I read a cookie cookbook and it recommended the latter approach. But as I said, I'm not much for jigsaw puzzles.

- Try it the other way to see how it feels. Pattern-matching is totally math.

- Don't want to bake or do more crafts? How about just doubling (or halving) a recipe for dinner? Can you do that with a box-mix? What does ½ an egg even mean? (Hint, scramble it first, then divide.) Fractions are part and partition (heh, heh) of daily life!

- Have a big yard to mow? You probably know how long it takes… and somewhere you have recorded the size of your property (you can look on GoogleMap and estimate, if it's not handy to find those numbers). Can you figure out the rate at which you mow? How long per ten square feet? (This might come in handy when Grandma is trying to talk you into mowing for her… is it worth your time to do it or your money to hire her a lawn service? If you're feeling time-crunched and it's going to take you five hours a week… you might have a different answer than if you think it will take two. Don't forget she'll have weird things to mow around or weedwhack after you arrive… add a half-hour or hour to your private estimate.)

- How about all that driving you do every week? Is it worth speeding to shave five minutes off each day? Yeah, that's about half an hour a week, but does five more minutes at home (or work) really gain you anything… is it a useful chunk of time? How about playing with a map to see if you can find a better path? Or Looking at your playlist and adding up song-times so you *exactly* fill your driving time?

- What about running a bake sale or a craft fair… or even helping your kids with a car wash? The budgets for these things are usually pretty straight-forwards (you just have to record things meticulously) …and someone's got to do it. Why not you?

- Maybe you run a small business – or would like to. There's a good chance you're going to pay an accountant to make sure everything is on the up and up… but if you feel up to prepping a bit more of your records, you can probably shave off some of the hours that you're paying for.

Practical things you can do – without having to build a doghouse or make Princess Rose's blue ballgown from Disney's *Sleeping Beauty* which isn't available in stores (yes, my oldest daughter was obsessed and it was amazing and I was exhausted… but there are only pink versions in stores) – that use math abound in your life. You've probably been doing a number of them without noticing: everything from playing with the timer on your coffeemaker to counting the seconds for a red light.

The question is, can you look at all those things and see *opportunities* instead of *annoyances?*

And my answer is: YES, YOU CAN.

It's all about attitude.

And *that* you have control over…

(Unlike the sensor-triggered red light that only works when there's a car in the *left* turn lane and you need to go *right* … and it starts to become worth turning left and going around the block… Do I sound bitter? I'm just gonna say that an electronic sensor at a university-owned parking garage right next to the Engineering School oughta do better…)

Chapter Five:

Transitions and Sideways Thinking (Defeating the Fear at its Source)

- **Division, fractions and negative numbers**
  - **Don't lie: the truth about negative numbers and dividing by zero**
- **Algebra (hint, you actually do it every day)**
- **Geometry (your secret weapon with math-avoiders)**
- **Trigonometry (only one shape, how bad can it be?)**
- **Functions (you use this one every day, too)**
- **Calculus – not just for whiz-kids…**
- **The Keys to the Kingdom**

ALL RIGHT. EVERYTHING I'VE TALKED about so far is about working to deal with the fears and aversions that so many of us develop towards math. If you start with some of the ideas that I've suggested early enough on – and deal with your own aversions –

you might be able to build up enough positive emotions in your little kids that they don't fear math from the get-go. Most little kids love counting and showing off their early skills at addition and so on, so it's more of a matter of nurturing that early interest (and not killing it off through Drill-and-Kill or your personal aversions) than of developing something that isn't there.

Some of Math is easy to work with: it naturally lends itself to hands-on work or segues nicely into other areas that are obviously useful (like multiplication to figure out how many boxes of tiles you should buy to redo your kitchen floor); intrinsically interesting, entertaining, or beautiful (like fractals or game theory); or isn't terribly challenging (like addition).

But some of it… isn't quite so easy to get your head around at first take.

In this chapter, we're going to discuss some of the most typical points at which someone (parent or kid) throws in the towel. They may continue *learning* math after struggling through one of these points, but if the joy is gone and they're only doing it to pass the next test… they will have a terrible time trying to realize the benefits of math in their future lives.

The thing to notice with each of these typical points is that they are *transitions* between one set of mathematical ideas and concepts and a whole different set, with the new set giving you more options to do more things and "conquer more mountains." Like a painting that looks different when you tilt your head to look at it sideways – or a piece of music that speaks to you differently when you're in a different mood – you gain a whole new perspective if you can make that "sideways transition."

It's important to note that, by the time each of these concepts is formally "taught," they've usually been sneaking into the previous bits of math that you have been comfortably using for some time. These "transitional concepts" aren't intrinsically difficult, despite how we often discuss them and worry about them. And after one *does* pound them into one's head (often by moving on to something else that requires using the "tough" concept as a *tool* rather than a *goal*) they become easy to use... but somehow, we never quite get over the idea that these things are *hard*. The person who felt stumped by fractions at age ten, will still often say that fractions are *hard*, even when they passed their High School Algebra class with a very decent grade.

We tend to hold on to traumas – even ones over math.

TRUE STORY!

A young man of my acquaintance struggled with math. He is on the very high-functioning end of the Autism spectrum, and his mom had bigger fish to fry at the early ages than dealing with *math*. When she had him evaluated at age twelve, her son was diagnosed with a math disability because he was so far behind *by comparison to school kids of the same age.* My suspicion is that this mom never told the evaluator that she had never really worked with her son on math because they had so many other things to deal with, though she likely did explain her son's place on The Spectrum.

It's embarrassing, right? Which one of wants to admit to a professional that we have seriously dropped the ball? Especially when that professional has the power to call in the Powers That Be that are can Get Involved with your schooling and parenting choices. That isn't just embarrassing, that's *scary!* (A similar fear kept me for reaching out for help I badly needed with one of my kids.)

So anyways, this young man (and I met him at about age twelve) proceeded to pack *twelve years of math* into the next six. At eighteen, he was ready for college, having completed Algebra II and Geometry!

In preparation for college, my friend had her son evaluated again. (Colleges will work with an IEP as well – your kid can get extra time on tests, quiet testing spaces, etc... but you have to do the legwork and get the evaluation).

This time the young man was *again* assessed as having a math disability – because he was slow compared to kids who had been moving through their math at the school-system-approved rate. (Remember that I've told you that my kids – including my Mathematician daughter – are slow compared to school-peers because we don't do Drill-and-Kill.)

Again, I doubt that the evaluator had a clue that this *brilliant* young man had packed that math into *half the time!*

My young friend went to a top university – and whatever math assessment that university did, they wanted him to re-take Pre-Algebra and Algebra. These things happen, folks, and NOT just to our homeschooled kids. The university had these classes available because a *large number of public-schooled kids* need them, not because of the tiny handful of homeschoolers who attend their institution. It's not a great shame – though it can delay graduation depending on the kid's major.

Well, my young friend actually ended up taking Pre-Algebra twice (the format of college classes that first semester defeats many amongst us – it's a whole new way of learning), then Algebra, Trigonometry, Pre-Calculus, and Calculus. He took Summer classes in order to keep moving, and he sought out tutors (I was one of them). He got As in every single one of those classes – *and he was done with all those classes before his 3rd year.*

My young friend graduated on time (i.e., in four years – something I didn't do!), and went on to get a Ph.D. So, clearly none of that slowed him down – even though he and his mom both felt terrible about having to 'repeat' those classes.

To this day (as best I know) this young man considers himself to have a math disability. Because he was twice evaluated as such. Because he took extra time on tests and had quiet, separate testing environments when possible. Because he got through his classes with tutoring. Because he was slower than others.

However, to me his ability to get through his pre-college math in *half the time* and then *finish college math* in such a short span of time, despite having to re-do one course suggests he is actually *highly gifted* in mathematics.

He got mad at me when I tried to tell him this. He felt I didn't respect his struggles for how hard all of that was on him.

And I do. I really do.

But what he – like my own children – doesn't appreciate is that math is hard for *everybody.* When we homeschool our kids, they don't get the daily comparison with twenty or thirty other kids in the same class to show them that they are actually sailing ahead. Many of them get this crazy idea (and – hello? – guilty! That was me, too!) that getting help from a tutor means they didn't "really" do the work themselves.

These kids (and maybe we did as well) ignore the fact that they are the ones who went in and took the test.

They ignore the idea that in the Real World there are almost never deadlines for answering an Algebra problem (movies like *Hidden Figures* and *Apollo 13* aside – NASA is its own weird culture). They ignore the way that they use math every day very capably.

I had to give up talking to this young man for awhile – and I will certainly never bring up the subject of math with him again. I didn't mean to hurt his feelings, but his deep trauma regarding math prevented him from looking at the facts and accepting what an amazing person he is with respect to this subject.

Perhaps he will have a transformative experience in his forties the way I did and realize that he really is good at math. Maybe he will even go so far as finding pleasure in math.

I hope so.

Let's take a look.

Division, fractions and negative numbers

There are a few people who don't recall feeling like a brick hit them in the head when they were introduced to at least one of these concepts in Elementary School. I remember feeling like that myself.

And it's not really clear to me *why* that is true, now that I've taught these ideas to six of my own kids and had to look back on the whole process.

Part of the problem *may* be that we introduce them as completely separate concepts from addition, multiplication, and subtraction. They aren't, really. Just like multiplication is just repeated addition, division is just repeated subtraction… and I know this particularly well right now, because I am currently trying to break my 15-year-old and my 10-

year-old from using addition and subtraction instead of multiplication and division. The 10-year-old needs to do it the other way around to learn the technique. The 15-year-old needs to because he is using math as a tool for Physics and his no-multiplication/no-division approach is seriously slowing him down and (now) frustrating him as he works on Physics problems.

The Waldorf (or Rudolf Steiner) Schools introduce "all Four Processes" – addition, subtraction, multiplication, and division – simultaneously instead of one-by-one, and they seem to have fewer kids terrified of division. (Though that's just my anecdotal observation.) I have no idea how their students feel about fractions and negative numbers, but the idea of *simultaneous introduction* should give us something to think about.

If introducing division right alongside addition makes it *easier* for kids to cope with... then that suggests that there's something about the way we talk about division that makes it hard more than the subject itself. Introducing it right alongside makes it "just another thing" and not a big, scary *"now* we are going to do this really complicated thing".

But how does that work? Well, for details on the Waldorf approach I recommend the books by Melisa Nielsen (A Journey Through Waldorf Homeschooling). Even if you don't particularly get excited by the classic Waldorf approach of using a story about gnomes or squirrels (recommended by Donna Simmons of Christopherus) to get your kid comfortable with these "Four Processes," these and other Waldorf-based resources will give you a great deal of food for thought. (A nice side-note is that many of these approach-based resources are extremely affordable.)

For now, let me make the following suggestions:

- Use food to talk about division and fractions. Pies – including pizza – are always popular for this, but really any food that has to be shared out will work. You may not want to count out the French fries (eat them before they get cold!) or the peas — though your kids might — but figuring out how many whole (or partial) baked potatoes everyone gets, or how to cut up the brownies equitably can be very handy.

A warning on this one — some kids get absolutely *obsessed* with food-portion fairness. You may find yourself buying a small kitchen scale to soothe the highly picky, or trying to slice a cake into precisely equal sevenths. Have the kids do as much of this extra nonsense as possible. It will both be more memorable and reduce your labor. Remember the old trick of "I cut, you pick" to arbitrate fights over whether one piece was bigger.

- Use money to talk about negative numbers. This is one of the most valuable reasons for giving a kid money for an allowance or chores. They get very bought into having *earned* that money, so they get to spend it (within reasonable limitations that you set). But… inevitably… they will want to purchase something that costs more than they have with them — or maybe more than they currently possess. Perhaps you will lend them the difference — or perhaps a sibling will do so. It's important that *someone* does to get this particular point across: that they *owe someone back* a specific dollar amount. You *will* have to make sure the repayment takes place in a timely manner.

  That is a lesson in negative numbers that will absolutely never be forgotten — for both the borrower and (if another sibling antes up) the lender.

  And, honestly, that is a lesson that we would all rather our kids get deeply into them when they are five or eight and the most they are going to owe is a few dollars… and long before they have access to their own credit cards and can create a problem for themselves that takes more than washing an extra load of dishes or sweeping the deck to clear up!

I'll give you one more thought about divisions, fractions, and negative numbers before we move on. And this one is because this one hit me very hard, personally.

Don't lie: the truth about negative numbers and dividing by zero

When I was taught about subtraction, I was told that you "couldn't" subtract a bigger number from a smaller one.

When I was taught about division, I was told that "couldn't" divide by zero.

The only thing either one of those statements ever did for me was to make later stages of math more painful. The definition of *"cognitive dissonance"* – that lovely buzz-phrase – is that your brain has to accept as true something that it *knows* to be false. Usually this is because we were *lied to* at some point. Quite likely by well-meaning people who thought that either they were being helpful *("it's too complicated to explain infinity to little kids")* or who genuinely thought the wrong thing was right… probably because *they* were lied to about that issue themselves.

But cognitive dissonance is *painful*. Sometimes *physically* painful because that "deep truth" had become something intrinsic to our entire worldview.

A bit dramatic for math?

Maybe…

But you don't know how your kid (or your *other* kid, regardless of what the first one did) will look at it. We base our worldviews on things that are often not explicable to others, and we don't usually *know* all those bases on a conscious level. If you can avoid creating painful cognitive dissonance for your kids… it just makes sense to do that.

And while many of us may never have to deal with division-by-zero (those of you whoa re old enough may remember that it became a Big Deal when Intel rolled out their new Pentium processor in the early

1990s), pretty much all of us will have to deal with negative numbers in our daily lives. Those bills don't pay themselves, no matter how many of them you put on auto-pay! (Sigh…)

And this is true of so *many* concepts in math as you help your kids move forwards. Get used to saying "I'm not sure, let's look it up" rather than "that's not allowed." Find a friend who knows more math and ask the question. Model for your kids that *getting help* is most definitely *allowed*. Let them see that it doesn't matter what path you took to learn that information… but what you did with it after you learned it and it was yours.

So, what is the truth about division-by-zero and negative numbers?

Negative numbers are just owing. That's usually simple enough.

My son bought a toy at the bookstore and I agreed to pay half the cost, but his money was at home. My share of it was a negative number until he paid me back. (He wanted a book, too. I covered that one entirely.)

Or, going the other way, last Christmas, my mother-in-law sent giftcards for Barnes & Noble to all the kids. When we went to the store, we ended up pooling all the cards to make checkout easier (and having easily losable giftcards with just a dollar or two floating around). So, my then-9- and 11-year-olds spent the drive home calculating how much money I owed each of them – taking into account their share of the sales tax!

(In my book, *The Homeschooling Parent: Self-Care and Feeding of the Person Who Makes It All Happen,* I discuss the question of how to get chores done by using – or not using – money. I also discuss my unforgettable method for teaching decimals using a penny, dime, dollar, $10-bill, and $100-bill… and how to use coins to get them very, very comfortable with multiplication by 5s and 10s by paying them in small coins and then having them "trade up" to get fewer coins/bills.)

Division-by-zero is just as simple.

As the lower part (the *denominator,* which means the *name*) of a fraction gets *bigger,* the value of the fraction gets *smaller.* We all know ½ of a pizza is more than 1/8. If you keep making the bottom get bigger and bigger and bigger... the size of the entire fraction gets smaller and smaller and smaller... and eventually turns into zero because it's so small that it doesn't make sense to worry about it. If you put every kid's favorite "number" on the bottom – infinity – then it really is zero.

Putting a zero on the bottom is the same thing, but in reverse. One and a half pizzas (3/2) is bigger than ½ pizza. That's making the top bigger, of course, not making the bottom smaller. But if you now look at 3/1 pizzas (that's 3 pizzas, each "cut" in one piece) and that one is bigger than 3/2 pizzas. It's a little weird for some of us to put numbers *smaller* than 1 in the bottom part of a fraction, but it's perfectly legal. And as that number on the bottom gets *smaller* the entire fraction gets *bigger,* just as 3/8 is smaller than ¾, which is smaller than 3/2, which is smaller than 3/1. If you put 0.1 in the bottom (3/0.1) then you get 30, which is bigger still!

So, if you put the *smallest* "number" in the bottom – zero – then you have the largest "number" ...infinity.

(For you sharp-eyed types, yes, I am implying something is weird about calling zero and infinity "numbers". Undoubtedly some math-afficionado will read this book and sneer if I don't do that. If you want to get super-technical, zero and infinity are *ideas,* not actual *numbers.* For most of us – and certainly up through Calculus – it really doesn't matter. But since this whole section is about *not lying,* I decided to be honest about it with you. And if you let your kids in on this "secret" they are going to think it is the *best thing ever...* though you will have to deal with mischievous arguments about whether or not they ate their peas because they ate *zero* peas and *zero* isn't a number so... Which can get frustrating after a few days and until they wear out on it, but they – and you – will never forget that zero and infinity are ideas... and that is a super-cool thing to know!)

On to our next *transitional* problem-child:

Algebra (hint, you actually do it every day)

Yeah, I mean that. You use Algebra every day without thinking about it or noticing.

Before we get into that, let's go back to how most of us taught our kids (or were taught) addition and subtraction, multiplication and (maybe) division.

I'm referring to "fill in the blank" problems.

Almost certainly you (or your kid) were not faced *only* with this kind of problem:

$$3 \times 2 = \underline{\quad}$$

But probably this kind as well:

$$3 \times \underline{\quad} = 6 \text{ or } \underline{\quad} \times 2 = 6$$

The blank might have been an empty box, you might have had to write your answer next to it rather than in or on it, you might have had to fill in a bubble-sheet or click an option, etc. But essentially the same things.

In your day-to-day life, you-the-adult have a lot of fill-in-the-blank problems to do, such as:

30 guests for Thanksgiving Dinner x ½ pound of turkey each = ____?

Which could also be…

30 guests for Thanksgiving Dinner x ____ pounds of turkey each = 26 pound turkey

(If you're really getting into this, you might notice that I have reframed a *division* problem as a *multiplication* problem. It's the same work, but I still have lingering Issues over division as well, and this feels more comfortable to me. You'll notice in higher level math (Calculus and beyond) that there are a great many people who are "good with math" who will leave divisions until the very end of a problem. That's why you see fractions floating around all over the place; no one actually wants to do the *division* and they're hoping it will work out so they don't have to. Yes, fractions are easier than division. Even for those who like math.)

I'm sure that a little thought on your part will generate a few dozen more examples. But pretty much *any* financial form you have to fill out, or any invoice you have to prepare is a fill-in-the-blank problem or set of problems. Computers make this stuff simpler (when they don't make it harder) by doing the actual calculations, but figuring out which number to put where is usually a human-problem.

And now... (drum roll please)... here's the connection with Algebra.

They are the *same thing*.

A "variable" like x or y is absolutely the exact same thing as a blank line or a box.

Absolutely, *precisely*.

So, if you and your kid managed to wrestle past

4 + ___ = 9 you can do 4 + x = 9.

The level of "abstraction" that it takes to understand that ___ isn't really any different than it takes to use an x there instead. If it helps, tell your kid that X marks the spot where the treasure is hiding and they have to dig it up. Or that X is covering up the blank spot and if they figure out what's underneath, they get to get rid of the X (you can use Post-It Notes or some tape and paper to actually cover up

93

an answer… or some brilliant person probably has a beautiful, well-crafted manipulative out there for sale… MarcyCookMath.com cards are reasonably close to that, actually).

Next question: if we're already *doing* Algebra, but calling it Arithmetic… why does my kid (or I) have to learn Algebra?

A great question, and there are a couple of answers that I hope will satisfy you.

1. **Algebra lets you think about *how* to solve a problem without worrying about the details of what that problem is.** It's just like having a set of measuring cups in the kitchen: you can use them to bake a cake or brownies or to measure ingredients for slime or playdough. The tool is the same and it can be used to solve lots of problems.

   Except for those of us who are super-minimalists (*not* most parents, no matter their personal inclinations), most of us like to have lots of tools. Screwdrivers and spatulas and saws and baking pans and paintbrushes and sewing supplies and… We may never *use* all those tools, but tools are often the very *last* thing we consider getting rid of when down-sizing. Why?

   Because a tool is more than a tool. It's an opportunity. It's imagination. It's a dream. If you are the person with the tools, you have more Things You Can Do… even if that's just lending your tool to a friend or teaching someone how to use it. That hot-glue gun can stick flowers on a hat or be used to create a structural support for some weird ramp your kid is making. Tools open up *POSSIBILITIES*.

   Algebra is a tool. Learning to use it opens up more possibilities for you and your kid.

2. **Algebra lets you develop the skills to think about how to approach *any* problem, not merely ones with numbers involved.** In this case, it's more like actually baking the cake. You know that you have to mix the ingredients in a particular order (there's usually a great deal of flexibility in that order for most cakes, but for the sake of argument, let's say this cake is strict about the order). To make that work, you need to prep your supplies ahead of time, organize your workspace, etc. As a very particular example, my grandmother's cupcake recipe requires a ½ cup of *boiling water* added right before everything is mixed, and you need to get it into the oven as *quickly as possible* once the boiling water has been added. If you don't, the baking soda goes kaput and the cupcakes are... erm... *extremely dense.*

And there's other problems – the butter has to be softened, but not melted. The egg and milk have to be kept from contacting the baking soda or they'll set it off as well. The milk has to either be buttermilk or soured by sitting with a few tablespoons of apple cider vinegar for an hour.

(I'm making these cupcakes sound laborious, and they are not. Case in point: my 18-year-old dislikes cooking, but he'll make them for a birthday when I'm tired. They are also insanely yummy, and I have gotten people who told me they hate cupcakes to ask me for the recipe. If you want this recipe, you'll have to join my newsletter by emailing me at RisingDragonBooks@gmail.com or clicking the Newsletter Link https://www.RisingDragonBooks.com – put *Homeschooling Cupcake Recipe* in the subject line!)

You don't have to use Algebra as your tool to learn this kind of linear, step-by-step thinking. Computer programming (or even "coding") will help as well.

And you *can* learn it by doing other complex projects, like sewing a Halloween costume or building a doghouse or creating a garden or organizing a large social event (or baking most cupcakes).

However... many of those other kinds of projects will not *require* you to be quite so precise in the order of your steps and the preparation that must be made to get you to your final product. And *all* of those other projects will go more smoothly if you *already* have a very solid grasp on linear, sequential thinking and planning.

There certainly *are* other ways to approach a project... and as an artistic person myself who usually has about a dozen different things going on (and scheduling the kids) I am well aware that there are other ways to get things done. What I have found however – and I challenge you to look back at your own life and consider whether you have discovered the same thing – is that you can only go on for so long in a scattershot, "unconstrained artistic" approach. Eventually you have to pull in all the strands of the fabric before they unravel and knot them together in some way that is logical enough to hold. That might be collecting your receipts for your art business (and I am behind on that right now myself) or setting aside time to fold and put away the piles of laundry or books that are threatening life and livelihood (guilty again... maybe when I finish writing this book...). Or it might be doing a serious evaluation of all your paints before launching yourself into that amazing new project and then running out of Pine Green halfway through your second tree (reminder to self... check the paints...) or realizing that you really *don't* have the time and energy to bake cupcakes for your kid's birthday and you need a backup plan *STAT*.

There are, of course, always the Other Reasons you might be learning (or re-learning) Algebra with your kid: it's required by your state/district; it's required by a custody agreement; it's a requirement for something else your kid wants or needs to do, like go to college, get an apprenticeship, and so on.

But if you know what you are going to get out of it that isn't all about what other people need and want, it has more appeal. And knowing that you've really been doing Algebra since the kid hit addition…

It's only bad if you decide to let it scare you.

Geometry
(your secret weapon with math-avoiders)

Geometry also requires a bit of a mental flip. And for the kid who actually *adores* numbers and Algebra, it can be a rough transition.

But here's the awesome thing. Kids who passionately *hate* numbers and Algebra may – if they can stop just defining anything that is MATH as worthy of loathing – actually *love* Geometry. I've seen this happen time after time, and not just with my own, more visual kids.

Geometry works on the brain in different ways than numbers and Algebra, and was, in fact, the *first* way that the Ancient Greeks approached math at all. They seem to have had some Issues with defining numbers (remember Roman numerals… shudder); they didn't have nifty little things like +, -, x, /, and = ; and they didn't have ZERO. Trying to do numerical math was a hideous, painful prospect for even the greatest among them. Even Pythagoras (of right-angle fame – remember $a2 + b2 = c2$? You will after going back through Geometry!) …*even Pythagoras* hated numbers. Supposedly he actually came up with his famous formula because he was trying to prove that numbers were useless! (Thank you to my teen for this factoid… we're still working on the idea of recording references…)

Many modern math curricula – like the Singapore Math and Beast Academy that we use – mix Geometry in to the earliest years. Competitions like Math Kangaroo and MathCounts include a great deal of geometrical reasoning.

Geometry leads directly into fun things like fractals and origami – in fact, Geometry can be involved in so *many* Real World activities that it's often the most accessible part of math.

That doesn't mean it's going to be easily accepted if you have huge math aversions (or a numbers-and-Algebra kid/parent). It just means that once you can get past that first, instinctive refusal, you may find it easier to keep moving forwards.

Math manipulatives were *made* for Geometry… though many of them (like Cuisinaire rods) are oriented towards using Geometric reasoning to help understand other math concepts. So, you mays till have to hunt around a little.

And if you're looking for more help, Beast Academy in particular uses Geometry to teach other kinds of math. If your kid is Very Visual… and likes to play with stuff… give it a try!

Trigonometry
(only one shape, how bad can it be?)

Trigonometry is really just Geometry on steroids, but the very title of this topic seems to terrify a great many people. Maybe they were really into the *Teen Titans* comic books where Trigon is a multi-dimensional demon-conqueror?

Relax, this "Trigon" has only 2 dimensions. Three in some Physics problems (but then you usually treat it as 2 twice… physicists are famous for oversimplifying things… for example, they have been known to "estimate" a cow as being a perfect sphere).

I'd say it's not trying to take over the multiverse, but really, it already has.

Once you learn where you can use Trigonometry (known by its friends familiarly as "Trig") it's impossible not to see it everywhere. And to start imagining new uses for it.

I usually try to get my kids interested (rather than fearful) of Trigonometry in a handful of ways.

One is by pointing out all the triangles everywhere in architecture – they do a Balsa Bridge Building contest at our local university every Spring, so they have some personal, practical experience of this as well. There has to be a reason why triangles are everywhere – and there is. You can drag a square or rectangle out of shape, but not a triangle (or a square that has a brace running between opposite corners, rendering the square into two triangles). And a 3-legged stool will never rock like a restaurant table– though you can tip it over.

Another way is through trying to shoot things with Nerf guns or Mouse-Trap-Catapults or whatever we're using. Honestly, Trigonometry (and Parabolas, which somehow fall under Algebra, Trig, and Functions all) is *super* useful for your military-enthusiast kid who loves nothing better than to shoot stuff. A lot of this stuff was used in Europe for a long time *primarily* for military applications. (And that's another hook to catch your kid…. For the pacifist, challenge them with the question of the ethics of mathematics that may have been developed initially for military purposes. To really have a serious opinion, they'll need to dig deep enough into how the math works to understand what else it's used for.)

And then, of course, there's building things. We have three goats, sort of by accident (it's a long story) and we've never put the money/ effort in to building them a really sturdy shelter. So… we have the "lazy man's problem" and end up building them an entirely new shelter every year or so (with lots of minor repairs in between until we get fed up and build new). To build something that even has a *chance* of standing up to goats – who do *not* eat everything (like my kids), but *do* climb and jump on everything (actually, *just* like my kids) – there must be a fair amount of structural integrity. And that means triangles.

Once you've *used* triangles casually – sticking an angled beam on top of something in hopes that it will brace – and figured out what did or didn't work well… they just aren't that scary. In fact, the kids have once or twice been sort of *offended* that I didn't properly explain that there was a way to *figure this stuff out ahead of time* rather than make them carry heavy objects around and make it up as we went along. (Yeah, and there's the scattershot approach…)

It's also kind of funky when you realize that every shape can be turned into a series of triangles and then figured out using Trig.

And seriously? How scary can *just one shape* possibly be?

Functions (you use this one every day, too)

This is the one that has been driving my 18-year-old nuts the last couple of years. He has insisted that we start teaching the younger kids functions *now* – the youngest being about 8 when he started this campaign.

Why? Because all "higher math" is based on functions. And, honestly, a function is just an equation with an unknown. Which they have been using since they were doing $3x\_\_\_ = 2$, right?

When my son first came across functions (in his Art of Problem Solving [AoPS] Pre-Calculus book, I think) it was presented in a way that didn't look like that at all, and he struggled. One of his older sisters had struggled, too. *I* remember struggling with this as well.

We love the AoPS series, but this one fell down in precisely the same way as every other book I've seen that covered the topic of Functions: it presented them as a New Topic, something that needed that mental sideways flip to be able to absorb. There were abstract discussions of Domain and Range and definitions that are accurate, but fail to get across the basic point that the Domain is just all the numbers that make sense to put into the equation (function) for the variable and the Range is just all the numbers that you would expect to get out from those inputs. The ones that "don't make sense are said to be "outside the Domain" and are usually ones that cause the function to turn into infinity in one way or another – often by a division-by-zero. (Which is NOT "illegal" – dealing with division-by-zero and other ways that infinity shows up is half of what Calculus is all about… and if only someone had told me that when they introduced "functions" to me… it would have made a great deal more sense.)

That's it.

That's everything you need to know about Functions.

…

Okay, not really. That's how they *work* and why they're not *scary* and how they really are the same thing you've been doing for probably *ten years* by now (if you're a kid) or longer (if you're an adult). Just like Algebra is really just fill-in-the-blank math, but with a few more things attached so it's more useful as a tool for the things you *really* want to be doing, functions are more than just equations with a domain and a range or we wouldn't bother giving them their own name.

Looked at another way, a "function" is just a set of actions (which might be adding, subtracting, multiplying, and dividing) that you use to get something done:

- A function of a computer program might tell the user to type a letter Y for "yes" or no for "no" – the domain of that function is Y and N, and the range is whatever the computer program does.

- A function that you probably do every week is laundry: the domain is your dirty clothes, the range is your clean clothes. Your dirty (or clean) dishes fall outside of the domain (and the range. Messing with how much laundry soap or what settings you use on your washer will affect the cleanliness of your clothes – that's sort of like changing the additions and divisions inside the equation.

- A function that your kids may appreciate is that if they do their assigned chores and academic work, they get time to play on their screens. The domain (the inputs) are their chores and assigned work, and the range (the outputs) is some amount of time on their screens. You can fiddle with what happens in between those end-points – where things have to happen or how, and those might adjust the outputs. For example, you might have a one-to-one correlation between time spent on those other things and screens, or that there is a two-hour limit if they get chores done but not academics (or vice versa) but no limit if both are done. Just like with the laundry soap and washer settings, you'll get different results if you mess around with how you use the inputs to determine the outputs. (No matter how much other stuff your sweet kids are doing and how nice they are, are you really okay with unlimited screentime? A whole 'nother book there…)

None of this is rocket science… though you could use it to *do* rocket science. (Hey, shooting off rockets! A great use for all this stuff and so much fun!)

Functions are how we get through everyday life. Tell your kids that (and yourself). They aren't scary.

Calculus – not just for whiz-kids…

Why am I saying such a horrible thing? What rational math-phobic person would ever want to do *Calculus?* Or impose it upon their poor, innocent *babies?*

Well, first off, I'm not really a proponent of *imposing* anything on anyone. Encouragement, leading by example, and showing people what their choices lead to (including a healthy dose of "do you want to have no choice but to dig ditches?") work great. Most kids – and most adults – respond better to carrots than sticks. We all have Big Dreams until something comes along to crush them.

And Math should *never* have the power to crush your dreams.

(Well, unless you're running a Ponzi scheme or embezzling or something… but you need a lawyer, not a book on homeschooling math, in that case.)

Math should have the power to *uplift* your dreams and help you bring them into reality.

That said, Calculus *isn't* for everyone.

The ideas of Calculus are, though.

What do I mean by that?

Calculus was developed to solve problems that can be pretty weird. Division by zero, for example. Or things that seem so simple that you covered them back in Algebra.

Remember the equation for a line: $y = mx + b$

m is the slope (or tiltiness) of the line.

But what if you have a weirdo *wiggly* line? And for some reason you need to know the slope at a particular spot... how do you figure *that* out?

Why would you need to know? I can be facetious and say for "reasons known only to Calculus teachers" but really... imagine you're looking at a graph that is trying to explain climate change or population growth or the car industry's projected earnings or voter turnout. No matter what your kid does in life – unless he *is* going to limit himself to fairly manual labor and not worry about the larger society around him – he's going to have to look at graphs.

And there's only two things important about a single point on a curve on a graph:

- The slope at that point (is it going up or down? Where is it going next?); and

- The area under the curve starting from wherever the graph started and going up to that point. (On a graph of population, that would tell you how many people have lived altogether up to that point.)

- (okay, the shape of the curve and how it compares to other curves on that same graph can be important, too)

Calculus lets you get answers to those questions.

Not to mention that it also lets you deal with that gnarly, annoying Division-by-Zero thing that you were so careful not to lie to your kids about back when they first learned division and fractions.

And honestly? Sometimes just getting answers to gnarly, annoying questions that have lurked at the back of your mind for ever is a reason for doing things. (In the last chapter I'll tell you one of my own stories about finding an answer to a gnarly, annoying question.)

The Keys to the Kingdom

- **NON-Sequentiality**
- **SEQUENTIALITY & LOGIC**
- **FEARLESSNESS**

Math gives you so many opportunities that it's not a subject any of us can ignore for very long.

As I mentioned back in Chapter Two, the single strongest predictor of whether a college kid who *wants* to study Engineering manages to do so successfully is how they do in Calculus.

Your kid may not have that as an ambition, but in today's economy there are fewer and fewer make-a-living-wage jobs that don't require at least an understanding of when and how to apply mathematics – whether they end up doing it themselves or finding someone to do it for them, at least they will *know* when it can be useful.

As a writer, I'm discovering that I use math regularly. Some of it is more or less by choice – I'm a little obsessive about making the distances in my fantasy world make sense (I have pages and *pages* in my story notebooks of trigonometry…). And some of it is by fiat – since I have to do taxes and plan a budget just like every other small businesswoman.

Being an artist doesn't get you out of needing some math.

Math is key to having the *personal freedom* to choose your own path and not let anything stop you.

My husband has "decreed" that each of our kids will complete the equivalent of a college semester of Calculus before finishing high school... so that no matter what they choose to do, they won't be *limited.* Being able to study Calculus at home also means that they can spread that "one semester" over two or even three; that they can cry on our shoulders when it gets hard (our older two are a three-and-a-half hour drive away... we can't give them a hug after a bad quiz no matter how we'd like to); and that we can do the Homeschooling Parent THING and step in to find them the resources they need... but are too shy or simply too inexperienced to ask for or maybe even to realize exist.

As I mentioned back at the beginning, I "can't" do Calculus anymore (meaning I'm not willing to put in the time to get my skills back). I've been reduced to tears for the sheer frustration of not being able to help my kid do something I *used to* be good at. Their dad has had to step in. We've had to find other resources, both online (mostly Khan Academy, Wikipedia, and Zooming with the oldest sister) and on paper (Art of Problem Solving, a set of Trig workbooks my husband located, our old textbooks).

I can't teach Calculus to my kid.

You don't have to.

Whether it's Calculus, Pre-Calculus, Pre-Algebra, or Division (not even by zero), there are resources out there, and there is *no shame in reaching out* to get them. Use Khan Academy or a set curriculum. Call up (or email, I hate talking to people by phone) your local school or university Math department and explain that you are looking for tutors or classes or resources. Post questions in your local (and national!) homeschool groups. Contact a Russian School of Math – if it's out of your price-range or driving-range, they may still have helpful suggestions!

The first person may be baffled (or even a jerk) but the second or third will have someone to suggest or a website to recommend.

When we decide to take an active role in our kids' education (whether we are homeschooling, afterschooling, private schooling or public schooling) we are making a commitment to doing that hard thing and making a phone call (I *really* hate phone calls). Or an email. Or spending an hour hunting the Web (or, be real, it's the Internet – *several* hours, including some doomscrolling time on your current social media addiction).

You may not *have* all the Keys to the Kingdom – I certainly don't – but you have the ability to *find out where they are* and help your kids (and you!) gain access to them!

So, what are the "Keys to the Kingdom" with regards to learning math?

• NON-Sequentiality

It *does not matter* what order you teach and learn math topics in.

Not at all.

Not one bit.

The things you run across that you don't understand will inspire you to either delve into the topic (and the stuff that usually comes before it) enough to get what you want… or to set it aside, knowing it's super cool but that you'll come back to it when you're ready.

Do you or your kid want to study Game Theory instead of Fractions? Go for it!

How about solving issues with a rocket you're building on the computer game KSP (Kerbal Space Program – it's beloved at *NASA!*)? Don't let the fact that you haven't learned Trig yet stop you! My kids were *obsessed* with KSP and solved some things by trial-and-error… my husband solved his game problems by looking up videos that went over the math and physics.

Do Fractals make your artistic soul sing? Technically you need Differential Equations (after Calculus) to figure them out… but you can learn a ton about them before touching a single equation! (Try the book *Chaos* by James Gleick for starters.)

And you don't need Linear Algebra to program a cool computer game – but my 15 year old's game-in-development is starting to get complex enough that he might need some of it soon to keep going. Usually that's after Calculus, too. Will he learn the math? Or set the game aside for a few years? It'll be his choice… and my job will just to help him see his choices and how to make them *his*.

• SEQUENTIALITY & LOGIC

Yeah, I know I just said *don't* worry about sequentiality.

Let me refine that: don't worry about it in the *order* in which you teach and learn things, because you can always backfill to cover topics you missed in Round One.

Do remember that learning how to think sequentially and logically is one of the longest term and most broadly applicable benefits you obtain by learning math.

• FEARLESSNESS

There is absolutely nothing to compare with doing something so *hard* it *hurts*… and then *conquering it*.

Math is a relatively painless and low-consequences situation in which to push for that outcome. I say "relatively" because we all know – most often from personal experience – that math is *not* a zero-trauma experience.

But most of us did not have an engaged and incredibly *brave* parent leading us and supporting us in learning math. Someone who could role model exactly how scared or frustrated or angry math made them – and how they were Not Going To Let Math Beat Them anyways.

In fact, they were *so* not going to let math beat them that they were going to learn to Love Math. In some way. For its beauty. For its excitement. For the sheer joy of scaling the mountain and looking down. For the opportunities if gave them.

Your kids have that role model.

It's *you*.

Chapter Six:

Putting it all together
(Creating a Math-Positive Environment in your family)

- **Real life math with the kids**
- **Math games with the family**

THE POINT OF THIS WHOLE BOOK is that it's up to us, as parents, to create a Math-Positive Environment for our kids.

There's a number of real, positive benefits to the kids and the family for doing so: there's less fighting about schoolwork; homeschooling (if that's what you're doing) becomes easier, and outside-home-schooling (if that's your jam) becomes more livable; the kids might even decide that they like math enough to let themselves follow their dreams to a career or meet an ambition that might otherwise have scared them off.

> **TRUE STORY**
> I helped a friend out for a while with school pick-up for her kids, and got to talking with her then-middle school-age daughter. This girl told me

about how she had wanted to be an Architect when she was younger, but she gave the idea up because she "wasn't very good at math" and it would be awful if she designed a building and then it fell on people and crushed them to death.

I was stunned and sad.

I explained to the girl that *in the real world* it's not just your math – or physics or artistic ability or whatever – that gets a building made. Someone else is always there, checking your work, your numbers, and able to help you fine-tune the project to meet safety standards.

In addition to someone (and I'm pretty sure it wasn't her mom or dad) telling this kid that she "wasn't good enough at math" – and probably teaching it to her in a way that made it harder for her to learn (wrong learning style?) – no one had ever heard her interest and found a way to reassure her about her very thoughtful, considerate worry!

(On a more disturbing note, this young lady had decided to give up on Architecture – because she "wasn't good at math" – and decided to become a teacher! People who think they aren't good at math teaching more kids… is *not* the best way to produce a Math-Positive Environment in a classroom!)

In addition to benefits for the kids and the family, however, we as the parent(s) can get so much out of a Math-Positive Environment as well!

- Being less scared of math gives us more control over our daily lives

- Having a positive attitude towards math prevents us from avoiding simple math-y tasks like paying bills, doing taxes, or volunteering to run an activity for our community group that involves collecting money and budgeting

- Feeling good about our ability to do math gives us more skills to apply to our own jobs, dreams, careers… or *opportunities* in general.

Remember, parenting – or homeschooling – ISN'T JUST ABOUT *THEM*.

It's about us, too.

We are growing and changing while we raise our kids – no help for it, since we're alive. As long as we're at it, why not *choose* how we grow and change?

TRUE STORY

I struggle with extremely acute acrophobia – there are some roads that I avoid in our very hilly area of the Ohio River Valley, because if I'm driving them, I *will* scream quietly the whole way, which unnerves the kids. I will also try to drive in the middle of the road to avoid the cliff-edge to my right, and have to keep a sharp eye for oncoming traffic on those twisting roads. One time I seriously thought I might have to call my husband to come rescue us from "Skyline Drive" (which is even worse than it sounds) after I turned the wrong way and there was a drop-off to each side… I found a circular driveway and managed to turn our 15-passenger van around, so I didn't call (that, and the thought that I would have had to drive back there with him to retrieve *his* car…). And I literally *wept* all the way up Pike's Peak in Colorado, through Rocky Mountain National Park, the mountain of New Mexico, and the Austrian Alps.

My husband has what he thinks is a hilarious picture of how I wouldn't go closer than 20 feet to the *railing* at the edge of the Grand Canyon. (And, no, I didn't hike it. I tried the Bright Angel [supposedly easy] Trail three times, got turned back each time by the first blind-turn, even though I could see the hikers thirty feet below where it doubled back. My husband ended up hiking it alone…)

I don't *do* heights.

But I made myself learn to climb up onto a catwalk in college in order to become a movie projectionist. (Stupid college students would sneak up there and dangle a roll of toilet paper down to cast a shadow down the middle of the movie… to get my qualification to run movies I had to be able to handle that.)

I've gone up on our roof to inspect the F=MA and E=MC2 that my husband and the kids painted up there. (Though *he* can clean the gutters, thank you very much.)

And I have climbed the fifty-foot-high *open metal staircase with seriously inadequate railings* at Lock 17 on the Mohawk River in Upstate NY nearly every year since I was 14 in order to get onto Moss Island. (Which has some of the most *amazing* landscapes you will ever see. Giant, glacier-created "potholes" of rock that form a fantastical, 3D labyrinth to climb and play in… somehow *that* doesn't bother me.)

Letting my acrophobia control me has kept me from doing too many things.

Some days I am up for fighting it...

...and some days I'm not.

But I tried *really hard* not to let my kids see how scared I was. I didn't want *them* to share my fear of heights.

It worked... and it didn't.

Some of them fear heights (there may be a genetic component to this problem...) and some don't...

And some of them are just *darned* determined that even though it scares them to be up high... they are *not* going to let that fear make the decision for them. (At least a couple of them were very serious competitive gymnasts, doing Giants and Flyaways on the bars.)

So, we've decided that we're going to do our best not to let our fears (of math) control us.

We've decided that we're going to look for the fun, the practical, the everyday math in our lives.

We've decided to create a Math-Positive Environment.

We've touched a little on the *how* to create a Math-Positive Environment earlier in the book, but let's get a little more detailed.

Of course we need to make sure they keep progressing, with the goal being to stay at or above "grade-level"... Keeping in mind that "grade-level" is an artificial idea that some group of people came up with and it may or may not make sense for our individual, unique kiddo at a given instant in time. But "grade-level" is what is used to assess where kids – including ours – are at in a variety of cases: if they have to be enrolled in school; if a judge in a custody case is involved in the homeschooling decision; in negotiating with a less-convinced spouse/co-parent; and, eventually, if they pursue a college degree, join the military, or decide on a certification/apprenticeship that requires a particular grasp of mathematics. Given that we never *really* know where our kids are headed (ask your own parents' friends if you doubt whether that is true), it behooves us to give them the best start into that nebulous future.

To love learning (because they'll be re-learning what they need to make a living for the rest of their lives in our rapidly changing economy).

To be interested in the world around them (ditto).

And to not be scared of what they are faced with learning… no matter what it is.

A Math-Positive Environment is a *Learning-Positive Environment.*

We've talked before about how to support the academic side of math. I mentioned a few curricula, and suggested trying (or creating) a math club or math circle. Even math camps and the Russian School of Math.

But that's still working from the outside of the family. All those sorts of things take what someone else has defined as math and your job is to support what someone else is trying to teach your kid in some way. What can bring math home and make it something that belongs to *you*, to *your kid*, and to *your family*?

How can your home-based Math-Positive Environment truly be yours?

Real life math with the kids

The first, and easiest thing to do is to involve your kids in the real-life math that you started uncovering for yourself in the last chapter. All those things you were noticing and trying out with math for yourself? You can do them with the kids.

However – and it's an important caveat – *keep it real.*

If your kids get the feeling that you're only involving them in order to seize a "teachable moment" or drag them off into a math lesson at the drop of a hat… they'll see it as the scam it is and you'll lose them. Not only for math, but for *any* learning activities (though you can win them back by telling them – in words – that you realize it was too much and you're not doing it anymore… though it'll still take a while to regain their trust).

I'm not dissing "teachable moments" – they are totally real.

And I'm not suggesting that learning shouldn't be 24/7/365 – it totally should.

But it has to be *real*. Because kids are even better than grown-ups at identifying a lack of authenticity.

For example, it's cool to take your kids to the grocery store and have them not just hunt down items for you but actually take part in decision-making. Comparison shopping is real math, and can lead to some great discussions about the value of favorite brands to your family, what else you might do with the money if you went with generic, the nutritional value of water vs. juice vs. Kool-Aid vs. soda, and so on.

My kids and I agreed that the *big* box of salad (15oz) was a better deal than the small one (8 oz) – because the price-per-ounce was so much better that even if we threw half away (well, fed it to our goats or chickens or put it in the compost) we were coming out ahead. And they pointed out that having so *much* salad around might make everyone feel less like they are taking more than their fair share and so more would get eaten, which was good for all of us (remember the cake thing from the last chapter? It's not always about getting one's own just desserts in our family, but making sure no one else feels like they didn't get enough… the number of containers with *one spoonful* of leftovers in our refrigerator is… insane).

And they were right. Everyone in the family *does* eat more salad now and we go through that big box most weeks, even though my oldest daughter, the family vegetarian, is off at college. (Even though they eat it like barbarians, just grabbing a handful of leaves and stuffing them in their mouths… but it's *greens* and no one is *arguing* … I've let this one go.)

Now, my oldest son is insisting we shop at the discount/bulk grocery, Aldi's, to save money. He even does the grocery shopping to make sure we do it that way... even though a third to a half of our grocery list is still specific brands that he has to pick up at our regular grocery (Kroger's).

If, however, after that initial *cool* shopping trip where we spent five minutes discussing salad boxes and they helped me decide on the big box, I had then handed them a bunch of worksheets involving prices and such... The kids would have seen it as the scam it was – just an opportunity to get them to acknowledge the use of some basic math in shopping and then drill-and-kill.

Kids – just like grown-ups – want to see that their input and involvement are *valued.* That they are *needed* and *wanted.*

Yeah, they know that I *could* shop without them. They know their dad *could* have built the goat-shelter last year on his own or replaced the front door without their help.

But they can also tell when their contributions make our lives easier or more fun or when they help us see a side of the whole problem that maybe we parents hadn't considered yet. Such as the idea that salad was seen as a *scarce good* and therefore none of them were willing to eat as much as they might because they didn't want to deprive their siblings or parents. How on Earth was I to know that they were holding themselves back from eating greens to be kind to family members? I mean, kids can be strange, but that has to take the cake! (And no, my kids aren't *completely* abnormal. Despite my joke about just desserts above, the problem with cutting the cake really is the normal thing of everyone trying to get the largest piece. Cake vs. salad... not a big surprise, I suppose.)

So... explain *why it's helpful* to calculate the actual gas mileage that the car is getting. Walk them through how to do it a few times... then ask them to calculate it for you because you're just not feeling up to it that day. You can even offer that if they want that to "count for math" that day, you're up for that because you could use their help.

Or have them do the grocery shopping (alone or together depending on ages and maturity). You can wait at the front of the store and veto anything too drastically different than what you planned... or you can just pay for it and roll with it. If your picky eater decides it's worth saving 20 cents on a can of chili and is *willing to eat the results...* well, you may have won *two* battles, even if you all decide to go back to your usual brand next time.

Instead of making *for* them or doing *for* them... and most especially planning for them... have them be part of the process.

I let myself get too far behind in sorting out bills to be filed – for some reason, this is my biggest Achilles' heel. I was ready to cry – no, I probably *was* crying – with the stress of it all. My teenage son and daughter were willing to sit down and help me sort it out. Just having them there helped, made it fun, and got the job done. They *knew* they were needed!

And, oh, yeah, they also got to see what all our bills look like, from utilities to credit cards to medical bills. It gave us a chance to talk about how much things cost, and how their dad and I make choices. Or, sadly, how we sometimes *default* choices by not "making" them until it's not a choice anymore... embarrassing to admit, but a great lesson in personal finance for my kids.

Taxes and family budgets are *spectacular* tools for getting kids to feel involved in math. And since pretty much every adult I've ever met absolutely loathes doing those two things, it makes it better for us, too. To the kids – if you are doing it with them – it's all an exciting new adventure (don't get too clear about how they'll be doing these for the rest of their lives).

Remember, they are just *helping* us, so it's not the kind of chore it is for you and me... because they can *stop* when they get tired and we'll finish it up. Just like it's easier and sometimes even fun to go organize someone else's space than your own (or your kids'... I, at least, am usually too emotionally involved in dealing with my kids' spaces) *because you don't **have to** do it,* it's easier and even fun to do someone else's chore. Even if it involves math.

It can give the kid that great little emotional boost that they were *useful* and *needed.*

And it can give *you* a boost, because you weren't drowning on the Island of Evil Taxes all alone...

Just as with comparison grocery shopping, where prices are just the beginning of discussions that can include nutrition and the treatment of farm workers (or not), taxes and the math required to do them can be just the beginning of a discussion of the federal budget, homelessness, or even the nation's military policy. Homeschooling is almost *never* One Subject at a Time!

So... when you're looking for those "teachable moments" you should really be looking for the reverse. Which moments are *not* "teachable"? For example, when people (kids or parents) are exhausted, hungry, or have just had a bad day. Avoid those, and the rest (99%) should be your "teachable *life.*"

Now, the flip side of this is that doing Real Life Math with your kids means you have to be open with them about matters of budget or taxes or your planning process, whether it's planning a party or a costume or your "ten-year plan" (because we all have one of those, right... I wish...)

Not all of us are comfortable doing that sort of thing.

There *are* a lot of benefits to talking about home finances and planning and goals, of course. I've been told that the uber-rich talk about money all the time and their kids learn to talk about it comfortably – whereas those of us who are struggling talk about it all the time, too, but in a "money sucks" kind of way, and those of us in the middle don't like to talk about it at all. If the uber-rich really *do* talk about money around and to their kids – well, it's something to consider for the rest of us. Even if we don't really *like* money… we don't want our kids to be so dismissive of it (or scared of it) that they don't make enough to survive more than hand-to-mouth.

But it's not *easy* for a lot of us.

My parents argued about money a lot, so it's hard for me because my stomach gets tight and I feel sick – part of me can't help remembering those scary arguments (which honestly weren't *that* bad – they loved each other dearly, but they both came from argumentative families and… it got *loud*). My in-laws didn't share a lot about finances with their kids, not wanting them to worry, so they didn't talk about budgeting in front of my husband and his sibs. The result of this is that my husband and I more or less avoid discussing money… though we have a very similar approach, so we make it work for us (mostly).

But we have *both* made a *concerted effort* to talk more openly with the kids about money, including showing them our taxes and bank accounts and budgeting. (And since we don't talk well to each other, they are getting two different views on the same story…) And we've helped our older children do their own taxes when they started earning some money at their gymnastics coaching jobs and to fill out their FAFSA form (Free Application for Federal Student Aid). We've managed to teach them to read all the fine print for their student loans and bank accounts and even those EULAs (End User License Agreements) that show up with every piece of software and every electronic device. (My son actually read through the *entire* agreement *and* all the supplementary, linked pages when we setup his account at Chase when he was 16. It was some *800 pages,* and he learned things from all that reading that were important for all the rest of us to know, since we have all ended up as Chase customers. I don't think I ever read *all* of it when I set up *my* account with them as an *adult*. He took one for the team… so I actually paid him for his time on that.)

My point here is that I get it. It can feel uncomfortable and awkward to talk about money to *anyone* and the moreso your kids, who don't have a sense for where the boundaries are on what's okay to ask.

Or what makes sense – so they'll ask something that makes you have to rethink everything you're doing and… maybe it's good in the end, but man it's *not fun* while you're sorting it out.

If you can't (or don't want to) get kids into your Real Life Math, there is another option.

Math games with the family

This isn't a *bad* option by any means, but it's definitely a different situation than engaging them in the life you're already living. Most kids *love* to play games with their parents, but unless it's an entirely *cooperative* game, the fact that you know math better might put them at enough of a disadvantage that it's off-putting to them. You know your kids better than anyone – so you'll know if competition or cooperation is the way to reach their little souls. (Real Life Math tends to engage them from the cooperative side just by its very nature.)

The rules for playing math games with the family are:

1. It should be *fun*

2. Math should be a required part of the whole thing

3. It should not be a thinly disguised drill-and-kill… if that's part of it, it should be right out there to see

4. It should be fun

5. Everyone – ideally – should be able to play… huge age differences can make this a challenge

6. At least one parent – and preferably both or all the adults involved with the kid – should participate at least occasionally

7. It can't be required (or it's not fun anymore), and…

8. It should be fun!

Games that aren't fun don't get played again. They get put on a backshelf (if you're lucky), and (if you're not) they discourage everyone from playing *anything* together in the future.

The good news here is that almost every game has some math component to it. Youa re keeping score, or strategizing, or matching patterns at the very minimum. Let's look at a few by category:

- **Card games.** These almost always employ a great deal of strategy and a fair understanding of probability. People who get *good* at *Poker* or *Euchre* or even *Rummy* or *Go Fish* have to understand what is the likelihood of the card they want showing up when they want it. Obviously, there's more of that in *Blackjack* than in *Old Maid,* but you can start with easier games and bring in more interesting ones as your family's skills grow. *Uno* is more along the lines of *Go Fish* in terms of how math-y it is, but it can be a start as well.

  Sleeping Queens is a fairly new game that is pretty blatant about its use as a math-tool – but kids seem to love it anyways... and it's just interesting enough to keep older kids or adults' attention for a couple of rounds.

  Charty Party is a relatively new entry into the field – it's like *Apples to Apples,* but you have to choose from your options which explanation fits the chart (graph) and then the "best" one is picked and awarded points. There are a dozen or so cards that you might want to take out before playing with your kids, but that leaves plenty to work with. The "explanations" are hilarious.

- **Boardgames or dice-games.** *Chess* and backgammon and *Go,* of course, but *Yahtzee* is a start and *Othello* is deceptively simple. We play a lot of *Monopoly* and *Risk* and *Axis&Allies* here – along with a number of other such things – and for the younger kids I count them all for "math"... for the older kids I have to get a sense that they learned something significant about strategy, but "Game Theory" is a valid branch of mathematics (so long as I'm strict with myself about what I count). *Ticket to Ride* and *Russian Rails* are also great games that require strategic thinking and some rather basic math. *Munchkins* is another one that might capture everyone's attention and with all its variations you'll find one that works for everyone.

- **Pattern-matching games.** *Dominoes* and *Qwirkle* are pattern-matching games that can be played competitively or cooperatively. *Sudoku* is usually single-player, but working together to solve one – just as many people do with crosswords – could be very satisfying.

- **Role-playing games.** *Dungeons&Dragons* and its intellectual offspring are actually a little weirdly math-heavy. It's all simple stuff – nothing beyond basic arithmetic – but there seems to be enough that it actually attracts the math-loving nerdy kids and repels a high percentage of the artsy ones who have convinced themselves math isn't their thing.

  Of course, there are some role-playing games (often science fiction-based ones that are about moving spacefleets around) that start to get into technical details and can get a bit more math-y... but even there, it's about the play, not the math.

The games listed above barely scratch the surface of math-involved games, of course. There are online games and extremely abstract ones like the *Game of Life* (its inventor, Dr. Conway, created a plethora of math games over his lifetime). If you look, you'll find them.

But here's a few other things to get you started:

- **Counting Cows.** I found this one on MinivanMom. com and it has been... weirdly popular on our car-trips. I can't rightly call it *math,* because it's just counting... but even the older kids seem to find it... fascinating.

  The simple rules are that the people on the left side of the car are a team, and the people on the right side of the car are the other team. You look out your windows and try to count as many cows as you can. *But* you also have a "spy" on your side watching out the other team's windows – if they see a graveyard on the other team's side, the other team's cows all "die" and they have to start over. Whoever has the most cows when the ride is over (or you pull into a rest-stop or whatever) wins.

I have no idea why everyone loves this, but it keeps them (relatively) quiet and reduces (usually) the fighting on long trips.

- **The Numbers Game.** I explained this in Chapter Two – just keep finding the next number. Best done cooperatively and over a span of weeks.

- **ProdigyGameOnline.** I haven't found anything else quite this helpful... and since the kids are all anonymized (their avatars have different names than them) they *can* find each other to play together, but they have to know whom they are looking for. Very safe, free, and since the homeschooling teacher/parent can assign specific types of problems or see how the kid did on stuff, almost insanely useful. My kids are under no illusions that this is about seeing what they know about math... and they still love it up through age 12 or so.

  The biggest downside with Prodigy is that unless you are *very* dedicated to the idea of playing with your kid... it's not really an adult-interest-holding game. (Of course, I feel the same way about Minecraft, and plenty of adults enjoy that... so maybe it's more me.)

- **MarcyCookMath.com** This first came to my attention from the book *Teach Like Your Hair Is On Fire* by Rafe Esquith – which is awesome for getting all kinds of ideas for teaching… just don't try to do them all (I'm not sure how Mr. Esquith, a 5th grade classroom teacher in a tough school in L.A., manages not to burn out).

Marcy Cook (also a former teacher) invented a "game" where the kid has the digits 0-9 as movable playing pieces and has to place them on a card such that it makes the equation (given on the card with blank spaces) make sense. There are sets going from basic counting up through pre-Algebra.

My kids – all six of them – have enjoyed these. It seems to combine the aspect of a puzzle with enough math to make it very, very useful. These can be done on one's own, competitively (who can finish theirs first?) or cooperatively… though that might get a little messy if one child takes over. One advantage is that the card-packs are fairly inexpensive, and have quite a few cards in each one – so you can keep re-using them after shuffling, and you can have packs on hand for kids at all the different levels you are homeschooling. Your 2nd grader can compete at her level and your 5th grade can do problems at his.

This is very blatantly *math,* of course… so use with some discretion. And remember, you should do some of them, too!

• Rhymes, balls, and jumping games. These work really well to teach counting, addition, multiplication, and more. You can do them on flat ground or on a trampoline.

There are a number of suggestions listed in Rafe Esquith's book mentioned above, but also in the Waldorf resource books, such as *Path of Discovery* by Eric Fairman. These sorts of techniques are used by Waldorf teachers up through the elementary grades all around the world.

- And even more blatantly math... This I what my family likes to do over Christmas. If we forget, the kids insist. Even the ones who aren't particularly *math-kids.*

  The name of the game is **Beat Daddy**... if someone else in your family is the math person, name it after them.

  What we do is have me go to a worksheet-generating site and print out customized math worksheets that are at each person's personal level. Yes, these are "drill-and-kill" worksheets. (I love Math-Aids.com... it's one of the few sites I have actually paid to get rid of ads - $25/year last time).

  We then set a timer, and everyone dashes to finish their worksheet first and most accurately. The goal is to Beat Daddy – or my oldest daughter, if she's home. The rest of us all kind of take it as a win for "our team" if anyone manages the feat. (Although I'm not sure if the kids count me on their team or not. I tend to be pretty fast at simple arithmetic, too... all those years of drill-and-kill that my husband and I did growing up!)

  I have to confess that I found a way to guarantee the rest of us a win: Math-Aids.com lets me customize the most godawful worksheets with exponents on top of exponents mixed up with division... The problems might be physically impossible to solve in the time-limit. And... the kids are scrupulously honest an fair-minded, so I was forbidden from doing that again.

  We've also printed off the same "1-minute" multiplication or division drills from the same site and given everyone 2 minutes... since we don't do a lot of this and the idea is to challenge us all, not torture everyone.

  However, this game gets everyone's competitive juices flowing. It's not terribly *stressful,* except for the one or two kids who think they actually have a shot at beating their dad for once. But it's a good way to learn good sportsmanship as well.

Don't underestimate your kids!

The ages given on the boxes of most games are based more around whether or not a kid is likely to try to eat the pieces than on the ability of kids to play the game. Try different things out and go for the most challenging and fun game your family can tolerate – why bother with infinite rounds of *Candyland* or Hi-Ho-Cherry-O! with your toddler when you can play Sleeping Queens or *Uno* and enjoy it more yourself?

Sometimes younger players (or new ones) need to play "open hand" (i.e., with all the cards or whatever showing for everyone to see) or even sitting on someone's lap while the experienced person plays. All the children in my husband's extended family learn to play euchre by sitting on a lap and suggesting a card from the grown-up's hand by pointing silently at it – sometimes it's worth playing their suggestion so that they can see how it all works (but not for deadly serious games, of course). The method has worked incredibly well and is being used with the 3rd generation now!

Whatever games you decide to play with your kids, stick to the rules given above. Have fun, do it together, parents/adults should play, and don't make it a "we have to do this" thing unless that really does motivate your crew (it sometimes works for mine).

And don't forget to play *other* games! For other subjects if you want – but just for fun and so that you don't just drown in trying Do It All. Take your time and have fun, even if you end up primarily Gameschooling!

Conclusion:

Enjoy it! Finding the beauty in math

WHEN WE GET STARTED HOMESCHOOLING, we often feel we need a curriculum. And, honestly, *MATH* is probably the one subject for which almost every homeschooling family actually *does* end up using a bought curriculum. I do!

And there is absolutely nothing wrong with that. However, no matter what curriculum you choose, there's only so far you can go in getting it to be "cool."

After all, you bought a curriculum to guide you and your kid through this unfamiliar math landscape and, darnit, you are going to *stick* to those guard-rails. Because who knows what's on the other side?

The problem is that it's like walking the paved nature trail at the state park. You can *see* all the cool places that the side-trails go, but getting off the trail seems pretty freaky. And then you meet someone coming back from one of those side-trails and they start telling you about the cool waterfall, and the exotic flowers, and the endangered species of snail that they saw... and, *man*, but they are tempting you...

Are you going to take that side-trip? Are you ready?

If not, you might still be hearing – or *feeling* a lot of...

"Math... is really boring."

No, actually it's not.

It's not just *how* we teach Math, it's *what* about math we teach.

Yes, it's important to be able to do Arithmetic. And Algebra. And simple Accounting (well, taxes and budgeting, but I had an A-thing going there).

But, face it.

That stuff is about as delightful as a diet of crackers and water.

Dry crackers.

And *plain* tap water.

Yuck.

Now, no one has made you eat like that, and if someone tried, you would have some very unhappy things to say about – and to – them about this diet. If they then claimed it was fine for you, because that was what they ate themselves, you would probably not accept that as a reasonable argument.

But you've probably been doing *exactly* that with regards to math.

Let's consider the field of Mathematics.

We teach kids all the "basics" but what do they get excited about? INFINITY.

No surprise there, Infinity is a pretty nifty concept.

Know what else gets them going?

- Fractals.
- Math jokes.
- Game Theory. (They *adore* The Prisoner's Dilemma)
- Rubik's Cubes.
- Maps (because the coastline of England is infinite...)
- Wonderful books like *The Boy who Loved Math* (a picture book about quirky mathematician Paul Erdos... or for older kids, *The Enchantress of Numbers* about mathematician Countess Ada Lovelace, who invented computer programming).

· Math puzzles (not super-trivial ones)… and knowing that there are math "puzzles" out there that even grown-ups haven't solved yet! How utterly empowering to tell a kid, "yeah, this looks pretty simple, and it seems to work, but no one knows why – hey, maybe *you'll be the one to figure it out!"*

What could be more exciting than the idea that they can do something amazing?

And what could be more fun than learning how mathematics (as computer programming) made it possible to create something as amazing as *Toy Story*… just a couple years after the STEM world was wowed by the reflections in the ballroom floor as *Beauty and the Beast* danced?

We've all been amazed at the beauty of a sunflower or a nautilus shell or a fern – and likely a lot of us have been told that the Fibonacci sequence (remember, 1,1,2,3,5,8… you get the next one by adding the last two) can be shown by those things? I first heard of that idea on the old PBS show *3-2-1 Contact,* where they had a segment about the "Bloodhound Gang" each week (kids who solved mysteries with math). But they never *explained* where the Fibonacci sequence was in those shells and ferns.

It wasn't until I picked up *Coincidences, Chaos, and All That Math Jazz* to help me with Math Circle that I learned where the Fibonacci sequence actually *is.* I was *so excited!* I'd forgotten how frustrating it had been to me, but after *30 years* it was so exciting to find out this answer!

(The explanation is that each of these things has a structure where if you count it in one way, you get a Fibonacci number and if you count it the other way you get the Fibonacci number preceding or following. For example, the seeds on the face of a sunflower form outward spirals in one direction, or inward ones in the other. The *number of spirals* in each direction will be consecutive Fibonacci numbers. With the fern-frond, I think it's supposed to be the number of leaflets on each side of the main stalk. The *Coincidences, Chaos, and All That Math*

Jazz book suggested using a pineapple to see this clearly, so I bought three pineapples and had all the Math Circle attendees work together to use colored yarn to mark the spirals down the side of the pineapples at our kick-off event!)

Fractals are exquisitely beautiful… they were bizarre and interesting and totally impractical, but fun… until some clever programmers realized how helpful they are with animation.

Game Theory helped people design the first not-too-smart AIs that were able to beat Chess GrandMaster Gary Kasparov and *Jeopardy* uber Champion Ken Jennings. But kids can get int it with learning why Tic-Tac-Toe is a "first-player" game… and then trying to figure out what other games they play are heavily biased towards the first or second player.

There is an entire field with *unanswered questions* that people are seriously doing research on that is all about Counting. Yes, *counting!* Tell me what little kid isn't going to think it's crazy cool that there are college professors still figuring out *counting!*

Math has a beauty – or a mystery, or a story, whatever you want to call it – that can probably captivate anyone, so long as they get to see the aspect that will interest them.

That aspect is *not* Arithmetic for most of us (and certainly not after years of Drill-and-Kill and lots of negative feedback). It isn't Algebra for most of us either (after more years of the same approach)…

But it turned out it *is* Algebra for my oldest daughter. Not that she figured that out until she'd studied a whole bunch of other math and came back to this. (And it's not "normal" Algebra…) If she'd lost her excitement about math along the way because of to much Drill-and-Kill or to little of seeing a number of other, cooler aspects of Math than the normal "scope and sequence" we feed most kids… she'd never have figured this out.

I lost what my mom always maintained was an early interest in math in just that way. And with that enthusiasm, I lost opportunities to go into a field that probably suited me better and where I could do more interesting things instead of struggling the way I ended up doing. But I was convinced I wasn't "good enough" at math... just like my young friend in Chapter Four.

To many of you, dear Readers, have tread this path in parallel with me (and my young friend). To many of us accepted a lower paying job because we weren't sure of our math ability. To many of us accepted a lesser *future* because we let that lack of confidence, that *fear* control us.

It took me all these years to be able to see the beauty in Math.

It's time to break the cycle.

It's time to give our kids the Math-Positive Environments we didn't have.

It's time to let go of our own fears and rise above where we thought we could go.

Hopefully this book helps you to do just that.

As at least one pro-mathematics Holy Book has said:

"Go forth... and *MULTIPLY!*"

Math resources list

(compiled from
the chapters of the book)

- The giant Homeschooling Math Curriculum Review Spreadsheet (not mine!): http://www.homeschoolmath. net/curriculum_reviews/

- *3-2-1 Contact.* PBS show from the 1980s. https://en.wikipedia. org/wiki/3-2-1_Contact

  - Lots of fun math-related trivia and information, including the "Bloodhound Gang" mini mysteries featuring a set of teens and a younger kid solving mysteries with math.

- AMC (American Mathematics Competitions) https://maa. org/math-competitions

  - AMC 8 can be taken up through the 8th grade; AMC 10 through the 10th grade, and AMC 12 through the 12th grade.

  - AMC10/12 is the first step on the math competition path to join the US Math Olympics team.

  - These exams are tough – great for the kid who needs more of a challenge.

- Art of Problem Solving (AOPS). https://www.artofproblemsolving.com

  - This company began by creating a test-prep book for the MathCounts competition… and then expanded and expanded and expanded. They now have online classes as well as the books (and they work with MathCounts). They expanded below 6th grade with the Beast Academy books.

  - We use their books after finishing the Singapore 6A and 6B Standards.

  - Their approach is DISCOVERY BASED. If your kid loves solving puzzles or understanding WHY things REALLY work… this might be a match. A little pricey, but these are not workbooks, so the re-sale (or re-use in the family with the next kid) value is high. You definitely want to buy the Solutions Manual, though! Every single problem is worked out, and they are definitely challenging problems!

- Beast Academy (BA). https://beastacademy.com

  - A subsidiary of Art of Problem Solving for 1st-5th graders.

  - DISCOVERY-BASED

  - My kids loved the comic-book-style textbooks but refused to use the workbooks at all. I had a friend whose kids went the other way, so test it out. Buying just *one* textbook/workbook pair isn't too bad in price… and then you can decide what to go back for.

- Bottles with no insides (see Klein bottles)

  - Video by Numberphile - another great resource!

  - https://www.youtube.com/watch?v=AAsICMPwGPY

- *The Boy Who Loved Math: The Improbable Life of Paul Erdös.* by Deborah Helligman https://deborahheiligman.com/

  - A picture-book biography of mathematician Paul Erdös.

  - A reassuring read for parents with kids who are on the Spectrum or otherwise unique, but have their own special gifts (they all do).

  - Clever math things hidden in all the pictures – lots of special prime numbers, since Erdös loved primes.

  - Erdös was so well-respected and beloved as a mathematician that all mathematicians proudly refer to their "Erdös number" like celebrities may refer to their "Bacon number". My oldest daughter will have an official Erdös number after her next paper is published!

- Calvert School.

  - A homeschooling online option of longstanding.

- *Chaos,* by James Gleick https://www.around.com/

  - I first read this book from the library when I was about 16 (and very not interested in Math). The ideas have stayed with me all these years – I bought a copy of my own when I was in college.

  - Without actually doing math, Gleick (a journalist, not a mathematician) explains how fractals work… and a bunch of other cool things.

  - Easy to read, small chunks – written for those of us who are a little leery of math, but know that we want to (or ought to want to) know more.

- *Charty Party.* Card game for adults… (Amazon link to game)

  - I ran across this *Apples-to-Apples* or *Cards Against Humanity* style game on FB at the start of the pandemic. The idea is that you are comparing the options on the cards to a graph that everyone can see.

  - In 2020 the makers were working on a more kid-friendly version, but I haven't seen it yet. (edit: I've seen this on Amazon… not had it in my hands - it's their "all ages" edition) You can enjoy the original with your adult friends or older teens… or triage the cards to make it closer to kid-friendly.

  - (Not really a way to learn about graphs, but maybe a way to make them more fun.)

- Christopherus, by Donna Simmons https://www.christopherushomeschool.com/

  - Despite the name, I did not detect any particularly overt Christian emphasis in Simmons' Waldorf-approach homeschooling materials. She is a trained Waldorf teacher who homeschooled her own two sons before returning to teaching in a Waldorf school.

  - Simmons does not cover math in a great deal of detail (at least when I was using her books), but she directs you to other resources. Her books are more in depth on how the Waldorf curriculum works, and form a good basis if you are using a Waldorf approach overall. Waldorf is a holistic approach, so the math-positive component doesn't really stand alone, but is part of a broader world-positive approach.

  - I used Simmons' books and recommendations as a cornerstone for the years we "Waldorfed".

- *Coincidences, Chaos, and All That Math Jazz*, by Edward B. Burger and Michael Starbird https://web.ma.utexas.edu/users/starbird/books.html

  - An excellent popular math book… and the one that finally explained Fibonacci numbers in Nature to me!

- Dual-enrollment

  - (look up ADMISSIONS at your local university)

  - Enrolling in college courses while still a High School- or Middle School-aged child.

  - Often inexpensive (compared to taking college courses as a full-time student)

  - Courses may count towards an undergraduate degree

- *The Enchantress of Numbers*, by Jennifer Chiaverini https://jenniferchiaverini.com/

  - Biography of Countess Ada Lovelace (the daughter of Lord Byron of Don Juan fame).

  - Ada Lovelace is the person who invented computer programming – the computer language ADA was named for her.

  - This is a thick book with lots of Victorian Era history, details about Lord Byron (so not for the youngest kids), and the frustrations of being a very gifted young woman who was actively discouraged from pursuing her creativity and math interest.

  - The 2nd Tuesday in October has been designated as "Ada Lovelace Day"!

  - (Yay for math holidays! Also check out "Pi Day" = 3/14, and 2-Pi (or "tau" day = 6/28))

- FIRST Lego League. https://www.first.org

  - FIRST runs 5 robotics competition programs: 3 Lego Leagues for kids of different ages (under 6, 6-9, and 9-14), and two full-on robotics competitions for 14-18-year-olds.

  - Children register for free, but the 9-14yo Lego team's registration is around $500/year at this writing (that fee includes the supplies the team needs in order to compete – all the Legos and parts and board for a 4'x8' competition surface). New teams may also need to acquire a robot and laptop to program on... but those resources can be used for many years.

  - The 6-9yo's team has a lower start-up cost, and a lower annual fee.

  - Competitions are somewhere between November through early January – and your team usually has several options to choose from. If you win a local competition, you may move on to State, and then to Worlds.

  - I've coached Lego League teams for nearly fifteen years (with a break in the middle when my kids weren't interested for awhile).

  - Getting a Junior (now Explore or Discover) team started is a low time commitment – 2 hours per week for 8 weeks will do it, and I include 10 minutes of free-play at the beginning, a 20-minute snack break (which usually included a discussion of the team project), and 20 minutes or so to play at the end.

  - For the 9-14yo team, we've found that a 2-hour session to discuss the team's research project and a 4-hour session for extended programming work well – so, 6 hours per week. And we meet for more like 15 weeks, since we have a bigger project to handle.

• As the coach, my job has mostly been to secure a location, keep the equipment organized, and keep the kid-crazy to an acceptable level.

• I do NOT build with Legos. Although I can program, I don't do so with the team – when they get snarled up, I ask them to walk me through their program, they almost inevitably figure out what is wrong as they explain it to me. (We do have a programming expert – my husband – whom we can call on if I can't help them enough. He gets called in once or twice a semester.)

• *Fundamentals of Mathematics.* see Great Courses below for details.

    • A video-based course for adults that goes over addition, subtraction, multiplication, and division in a non-condescending manner. A great refresher before teaching your kids... or something to let them watch and work with on their own.

    • The video is set up to have you pause every few minutes and work out a problem, giving you time to actually pause it. Then after you re-start, it works the problem out in a very visually-satisfying way.

• *Game of Life,* by Dr. Conway

    • (Dr. Conway passed away in 2020. He created many things like the Game of Life that are of interest to those of us who are not mathematicians and wrote a monthly column for some years in Scientific American for non-mathematicians.)

    • This site is one of many that run simulations of the Game of Life: https://playgameoflife.com

    • A very simple computer simulation that changes depending on the initial setup. A regular square grid has some of the cells "alive" and black. The surrounding white cells are "dead" or "empty". If a cell is surrounded by 4 or more live cells (including to the corners) it is overcrowded and will die in the next time-period. If it has 1 or 0 neighbors, it will die of "loneliness". If it has 2 or 3 neighbors, it will "survive". And if it has 3 neighbors it will "reproduce" and fill all the empty neighboring cells.

• The questions you can play with are if you can find a pattern that will keep regenerating itself – self-sustaining – or if you can find patterns that will die off or "evolve" int new patterns? And can you predict the final patterns?

• You can also do this on paper – the *Art of Problem Solving Algebra* book has a pattern at the top of each chapter encourage students to play with this.

• The Great Courses. https://www.thegreatcourses.com

  • Provider of audio and video courses oriented towards adults. The teachers for the courses have been selected because of a reputation for being great teachers – many have won teaching awards. They are speaking to an intended adult audience, so they don't "talk down" – which many kids really appreciate.

  • The *Fundamentals of Mathematics* course with Dr. James A. Sellers of the University of Minnesota was spectacular! (He apparently also has Algebra Great Courses!) My youngest kids (6- and 8-years-old at the time) found it very helpful as it went over addition, subtraction, multiplication, division, and fractions.

  • We got that one from our library for free – they are a little pricey to buy new, but The Great Courses does sales promotions a few times a year. (I also check eBay…)

- Hexaflexagons

  - https://m.youtube.com/watch?v=VIVIegSt81k

  - Just pure fun - and all the videos from this YouTuber (Vihart) are great resources as well! (She has another one on how to make hexaflexagon tacos!)

- K12. https://www.k12.com

  - A popular online homeschooling curriculum that is often available through your school district. Highly structured, is my understanding.

- KSP or Kerbal Space Program. Computer game.

  - https://www.kerbalspaceprogram.com

  - This game – beloved by NASA engineers – can be played on almost any PC. The Kerbals (weird little green people) are trying to start a space program. You get to design rockets, build space stations, and even go to their moon or send probes to other planets.

  - You can play it with NO MATH – my youngest kids started playing at 6 and 8. You can also use Math to do your Rocket Science and build better rockets (or at least ones that you can figure out why they failed).

- Khan Academy. https://www.khanacademy.com

  - TOTALLY FREE VIDEOS on math and a variety of other topics. (A couple of my kids took most of a course on animation, and some of them have learned programming or physics or chemistry in part on here.)

  - Fantastic for the video-learner.

- Kitten Math. by Kelli Pearson

  - https://artfulmath.com/

  - A series of workbooks teaching math through… kittens.

- Klein bottles

  - Bottles with no inside: https://www.youtube.com/watch?v=AAsICMPwGPY

- Numberphile (the YouTube channel) is a great source for entertaining math videos about all sorts of subjects!

- Kumon Learning Centers. https://www.kumon.com

  - In-person centers where kids can go for after-school instruction in math.

  - Workbooks available in most bookstores.

  - Focus on lots and lots of practice in each technique – the way most of us learned math and what is popularly called the "drill-and-kill" approach.

- Marcy Cook Math. https://marcycookmath.com

  - Cool manipulatives! Buy a set of digits (0-9) for each kid, and packs of cards at whatever level they are working up through beginning Algebra! The kid solves each of the cards – the equations only work if you put each digit in the right place!

  - Even my older kids think it's fun to mess with these. Fast and straightforwards!

  - Very inexpensive, though there are so many card-packs you can spend more than you plan… but you'll get your money's worth!

- Math-Aids.com. https://www.math-aids.com

  - Highly customizable printable worksheets for everything from preK through pre-Calculus. With SOLUTIONS SHEETS!

  - Free – or pay a small annual fee to ditch the ads.

- Math Circle. https://www.mathcircles.org

  - A math "club" that seeks to help children and adults explore and enjoy facets of math beyond drill-and-kill and the usual scope-and-sequence.

  - Circles may focus on one age range or on competition preparation.

  - I ran the Louisville Area Math Circle for four years – I'm happy to share my notes! Contact me for more information!

- MathCounts competition. https://www.mathcounts.org

  - Math competition for 6th-8th grades. The Chapter competition round (where Homeschoolers can join in) happens in early February. The State competition is in March.

  - Inexpensive to register, but challenging to prepare for.

  - Their goal is to get ALL KIDS, not just the "math nerds" excited about math.

- Math Kangaro competition. https://www.mathkangaroo.com

  - K-12th grade competition, happens in March every year, registration is by December 21st. Options for in-person and virtual competition. Connected with the Russian School of Math in some places.

  - "Sideways thinking" math – lots of pattern recognition and similar stuff that doesn't usually fall under Drill-and-Kill. More creative.

  - The exams are relatively short, and the fee is very small.

  - I use this to keep my competitive-minded kids engaged… and also to get a sense of where they compare to others in their grade.

- Math-U-See. https://mathusee.com

  - A visual/tactile-based math learning series that goes from preK up through Calculus. Videos go along with manipulatives. This is a whole-year curriculum… but again, high re-sale value!

  - Highly recommended by several people with kids who needed this kind of approach.

- MinivanMom.com. https://www.MinivanMom.com

  - Travel-games for the family

- MIT OpenCourseware https://ocw.mit.edu/

  - MIT (the Massachussetts Institute of Technology, yes that MIT)has put a TON of their courses online. You can take them for FREE, streaming hte videos and printing off hte homeworks and exams. You might have to buy the recommended textbooks - but some of them include the professor's notes-that-are-not-yet-a-book. This is a great opportunity for hte kid you can't keep up with… though if you'll at least watch and appreciate it with them, they'll get a lot more out of it.

  - And they have a ton of courses that are NOT math as well!

- Montessori.

  - An approach created by educator Maria Montessori in the beginning of the 20th century. There is a great focus on hands-on, independent, individual/very-small-group learning.

- OakMeadow. https://oakmeadow.com

  - Curriculum seller. You can buy the Whole Curriculum (aka Curriculum-in-a-Box) or just the parts you like (à la carte). The individual parts can be very inexpensive.

  - OakMeadow began from a Waldorf approach, but has migrated more to the mainstream to be more useful to more families.

- Path of Discovery (POD) by Eric Fairman.

    - This site includes a review of Path of Discovery and other Waldorf resources: http://www.waldorfreviews.com/eric-fairmans-a-path-of-discovery/

    - Books by a Waldorf teacher in Australia describing the details of the curriculum he put together as he worked with his class. Waldorf teachers begin with 1st grade and continue with their students through 8th grade before starting over with a new class – Fairman says he was surprised by how little there was in the way of guides for new teachers, so he put together his own guides.

    - This 1st-8th grade series is very inexpensive but gives a very good look at how to develop a Waldorf approach for your child. Fairman includes the little games and rhymes that he used with his students.

- ProdigyGameOnline.   https://www.prodigygameonline.com

    - K-8th grade and FREE. (Although you can buy a membership so your kid can do in-game purchases. My youngest asked to do this one year, but didn't ask me to renew it… and the membership is cheap anyways.)

    - Kids create a little mage-avatar (game character) who they then use to explore the world and fight magical battles against other kid-mages and game animals. Battles are done by casting spells – which work if they correctly solve a math problem. Battles end when either one of the kids or animals runs away (loses to many lives) or an animal is "tamed". Kids (and their tame animals) can level up.

    - As the parent you set up a Teacher account and you can see more info about how your kid is doing than you probably want. What kinds of problems, how many they got right, how fast they got them done, etc. You can see how those problems fit to US Common Core or various US state curricula, and what categories of math topics they fall under. The useful part to me (that Meenakshi had to tell me about) was that you can actually set assignments for your kids to make them have to use more of one kind of math or another.

• Every six months or so, the kid gets run through a "placement test" – which is more game play to them, but they get progressively harder problems over a few days of play and you get a sense of how they are improving. (All at once, instead of having to sort through all the other data.)

• The kids think it's just a game, so no fighting! I let mine use it in place of other math work one day a week… mostly because we're trying to reduce screentime.

• This is a great SUPPLEMENT and TESTING option, but probably not a standalone for learning new math for most kids. (Also, they can learn to game the system fairly easily…)

• Royal Fireworks Press.

  • https://www.rfwp.com

  • A homeschool curriculum provider focusing on the Gifted student market.

  • Both textbooks and online classes are available.

  • We've used some of their resources and enjoyed them. Reasonably priced for what you get.

  • Dr. Rachel MacAnallen, who writes their math curriculum, was a gamechanger for me when I heard her speak at a homeschool convention. She discussed a different way to understand subtraction… and I realized that my oldest daughter had come up with that method herself as an 8-year-old. Unfortunately, my daughter had gotten stuck and it had looked so odd to me that I told her we needed to do things the "normal" way… either saying or implying that her way was wrong. It wasn't… but I didn't know that until hearingDr. MacAnallen speak. My daughter was about sixteen when I came back from that convention; I apologized to her for not realizing that her method was actually better.

- Russian Schools of Math

    - https://www.mathschool.com

    - A series of in-person programs across the US focusing on the Russian model of learning math. As I understand it, they seek to build a math-positive attitude in kids through after-school classes.

    - Not as much drill as Kumon, and more of a focus on that "sideways", creative approach to math that the Math Kangaro test uses.

- Singapore. https://www.singaporemath.com

    - preK-12th grade available.

    - Affordable – buy just ONE workbook and textbook and Teachers/Solutions manual to try it out.

    - We use the Standards Edition (supposedly closer to the original program that came from Singapore) up through book 6B, then switch to Art of Problem Solving. Meenakshi tried the 7th grade books and wasn't happy with them and we haven't tried them on the other kids.

    - We use just the workbooks and I let the kids do just the reviews until they hit stuff that they don't know or can't reliably get over 80% correct. My youngest kids like to go back and fix their errors, but the older ones just wanted to keep moving forwards.

- Sleeping Queens. Card game for little kids.

  - https://gamewright.com/product/Sleeping-Queens

  - Blatant use of math, but engaging enough for both adults and teens (for a couple rounds anyways) and little kids (wh won't want to stop).

- *Square One TV*. PBS show from the 1980s.

  - https://www.youtube.com/watch?v=A-vPvGoB6YA

  - A variety show with game-show components, short videos, and more – all about math – that was entertaining to both me and my 10-years younger sister.

- *Star Wars Math* workbooks. by Workman Publishing

  - https://www.amazon.com/Star-Wars-Workbook-Grade-Workbooks/dp/0761178082

  - A series of workbooks teaching math through Star Wars

- *Teach Like Your Hair is On Fire,* by Rafe Esquith

- https://en.wikipedia.org/wiki/Rafe_Esquith

  - An inspiring book about a 5th grade teacher in Los Angeles. This is the teacher we would all love to have had… though I think I would have been utterly exhausted as a kid in his classroom. My family took some of his suggestions (like using Marcy Cook Math) and were simply awed by the rest.

  - I actually read this to my kids aloud, after my husband got it on audiobook to listen to on his commute. He's not a big reader, even an audiobook reader, so… yeah, it's that good.

- *Things to Make and Do in the Fourth Dimension,* by Matt Parker

  - https://standupmaths.com/ Mr. Parker is described as a "recreational mathematician, author, comedian" according to Wikipedia. This book is not listed on his webpage or Wikipedia page... Not sure why...

  - A popular math book. Easy to read, lots of interesting things.

- Waldorf/Rudolf Steiner approach

  - This is an entire approach, not just one thing.

  - Introduces addition, subtraction, multiplication, and division together in 1st grade. All concepts introduced through art and music. Lots of fun.

  - I wasn't as impressed as we got towards Algebra… but Waldorf resources go up through High School.

  - The curricula that I've used included Christopherus, A Journey Through Waldorf Homeschooling, and Path of Discovery (POD). OakMeadow began as a Waldorf curriculum, but has become its own thing... please look at the individual entries for these different curricula.

- Waldorf Essentials by Melisa Nielsen https://www.waldorfessentials.com/melisanielsen

  - Nielsen is a divorced-and-remarried mom with (last I knew) 5 kids. I "met" her initially on a Waldorf Homeschooling yahoogroup and got to know her as a contributer and then moderator before buying her books. I've never met her in person.

  - Nielsen's practical descriptions of how to accomplish Waldorf-approach homeschooling with multiple children on multiple levels was very helpful to me, as a mom of six myself.

- Her business has expanded tremendously and she now has options to help co-ops, pods, and charter schools as well as doing personal counseling. Her books include ones specific to grades, as well as a series of math books. (Caveat here: I haven't used her stuff since before she began this expansion.)

- More power to another homeschooling mama who is sharing her wisdom with the rest of us!

Also by Kerridwen Mangala McNamara

YOUNG ADULT Fantasy:

- ***Thony and the Much-Anticipated Adventure***
  Book One of The Prankster Prince

- ***Thony Goes Astray! (in the Deep, Dark, and Dangerous Fairy Wood)***
  Book Two of the Prankster Prince

- ***A Not-So-Sacrificial Maiden***
  Book One of the Knightess of the Realm

- ***Out of the Woods... Hopefully***
  A Knightess of the Realm Prequel

More YA coming soon...

- ***So You Want to Be a Hero***
  Book Three of the Prankster Prince   (expected Spring 2024)

FANTASY:

- ***The Rebel Duchess***
  Book One of the Chronicles of Ilseador

- ***A Not-So-Simple Mission***
  Book Two of the Knightess of the Realm

More Fantasy coming soon...

- ***The King's Champion***
  Book Two of the Chronicles of Ilseador (expected November 2023)

- ***A Not-So-Unexpected Problem***
  Book Three of the Knightess of the Realm (expected December '23)

NON-FICTION:

- ***The Homeschooling Parent***
  Self-care and Feeding of the Person Who Makes It All Happen

Author's Note

So… this book started out a little differently.

I've been playing around with the idea of writing a book about math for several years. The title was supposed to be "One Plus Three Equals Zebrapants" – which came from one of those funny misunderstandings that happen in the car when you're half-listening to the kids. My husband convinced me that no one would have a clue what that meant and, even with the subtitle, it would never show up on a search.

So there went my cute title. (And the amusing title image… sigh…)

Then I invited my oldest daughter, Meenakshi, to be my co-author. She was very excited about the prospect and agreed immediately.

Meenakshi is one of Those Homeschooling Kids that you see on TV – or she would be, if we were seeking publicity (but, OMG, that would be So. Much. Work.). There are a lot of snippets of her story in this book… but I'm her mom and I get to brag a little more here. She's graduating form Purdue University this Spring (2024) with a double major in Math and Physics. At Purdue she runs the Society of Physics Students and the Math Club, started a mentoring program for all incoming Math majors who want to participate (close to 100 per year), and is involved with several other groups like Women in Physics. She's published papers in Engineering, Physics, and Math, worked on research projects in four different states, and gets regular invitations to speak at major conferences. As an undergrad. At the end of her "Freshman" year (she came in with credits from taking classes as a dual-enrolled high school senior at her dad's university, so was a Junior by credits) she earned merit-based "Best Student" scholarships that were usually awarded to upperclassmen from both the Physics and Math departments at Purdue – and then went on to win the nationally competitive Goldwater and Astronaut Scholarships. She's currently applying for grad schools and a Fulbright Scholarship to study abroad... and taking classes in between traveling back and forth across the country to conferences.

And she has a boyfriend and rock-climbs in her "spare" time.

Phew!

It's probably no surprise to anyone that Meenakshi and I discovered that she didn't have time to be my co-author. (I'm still hoping to release a second edition with her commentary...)

And this was a kid who really could not have cared less about Math until she was about 14-years-old!

(Before anyone panics here... my other kids are awesome in their own ways, but they're not as super-focused on traditional academic subjects. And they tolerate math – and even enjoy it on occasion – but it is definitely not a passion. I anticipate that they will all go off and find their own cool and satisfying things to do with their lives... we're trying our darnedest to encourage them not to see their oldest sister as the person to try to "be like" except in the matter of finding what they love to do and pursuing it with all their heart.)

(And, yeah, like every other parent with a child who is highly achieving in the areas that get attention, we struggle with that...)

So... we'll see where this goes.

In other news, the next Homeschooling book is probably going to be about making it through the High School years (likely "The Homeschooling Parent Does High School!" or something similar). I touched on this topic in the first book... but it's one that comes up a lot and an awful lot of us get freaked out at that point and send the kids to school. If that's the best choice for your kid and your family –

more power to you! I just don't want to see you making that decision out of fear and the idea that you "can't" do it if you all want to keep homeschooling.

If that's not the topic you are struggling with, email me (or message me on FB) and let me know what you would like to see me write about! I can't guarantee a whole book, but I'm posting on my FB page and gearing up to a weekly blog.

If this book has been helpful to you, please let me know – and post a review on Amazon, GoodReads, Barnes&Noble, or any other site where you like to buy books. Something as simple as this following bit would work (and you are welcome to cut-and-paste this – but please leave off the quotation marks)

"This homeschooling book was helpful and easy to read. Mangala's style made me feel like we were sitting down together. I am much more confident about teaching math now!"

(And, of course, this is just a suggestion to get you started and how I hope you feel after reading The Homeschooling Parent Teaches Math! Please post what rang true for you.)

Until next time, my friends!

Kerridwen Mangala McNamara

P.S.

And for those of you who are driven crazy by cryptic dedications (and car license plates that clearly mean something, but you can't figure out what)...

The "Greenland marketing scheme" my husband and I began around the time our eldest child learned to talk was to begin telling her – and the rest, but you can see where the seeds sprouted – that "Differential Equations is the most fun math! We can't wait till you get to DiffEQ!"

I was hoping to convince the kids early that math wasn't scary — and, honestly, DiffEQ (as they called it at my college) really was where things started to get interesting and fun. Not so much so that I kept taking math courses after that, and it was deeply disturbing to me that I'd reached math where there weren't always answers, but it was, you know, cool. A big part of that was the professor I had, who clearly loved his subject passionately and confided it to us in this almost whispery voice as if he was giving us the greatest piece of magic imaginable. (I would thank him by name here, but it's been almost 30 years, and I've misplaced it, sadly...)

For the record, Meenakshi says we lied to her. There are much more fun branches of math than DiffEQ.

I may take her word for it. DiffEQ is where fractals are born, and that's good enough for me.

RisingDragonBooks

About the Author

Mangala spent most of her life as a Math-Appreciator, but definitely NOT a Math-Enthusiast. To be honest, her tolerance for Math has its ups and downs these days, and that nasty old Fear Monster bites her in the butt whenever she tries to help her High School Senior with Calculus. (Higher math is not like riding a bike…)

One of Mangala's major goals is for her kids not to share that Math Fear, however. Nor her fear of dogs and high places. All three topics are a work in progress with greater and lesser successes and failures, and aside from occasional nightmares about suddenly discovering she was registered for a college course she didn't know about right before Finals Week… it's going well enough that Child #3 (Calculus-kid aka Car-Guy aka "I hate math" Guy) was recently heard to be advocating for Math now being "fun" to a younger child and telling him to stick with it till the other kid gets there. (Note that Child #3 never said this to Mangala directly… it was passed to her through another sibling.)

You never know…